I M POSSIBLE

I M POSSIBLE

Tarun Kumar Pithode

Ocean Books Pvt. Ltd.
ISO 9001:2015 Publishers

Published by

Ocean Books (P) Ltd.

4/19 Asaf Ali Road,
New Delhi-110 002 (INDIA)
e-mail: info@oceanbooks.in

ISBN 978-81-8430-345-2

I M POSSIBLE

by Tarun Kumar Pithode

Edition
2025

Paperback Price
₹ 350.00 (Rupees Three Hundred Fifty only)

Printed at
Narula Printers, Delhi

For Naitik, Neeti,
Papa, Mamma and Kamiya

Preface

This novel is not about a story, but about a life, a life part of which I too have experienced and I do not intend to disown it. May be we are living in the age of possibilities where impossible seems to be possible quite often than not and thus, born a story which very aptly describes what today's youth is capable of achieving. Sitting in Bhopal, at a time when most of my friends were working in the field, and I was busy in learning new realities of life, I stole time, mostly from my family's share, to jot down few things, which I experienced in my life during my struggle, a struggle to become somebody from nobody, to share with today's generation and with a lot of people of my kind, who struggle, to carve a life full of achievements and to find their destiny. I have tried to present all in a story. I believe this novel, apart from being a story, will help people find their struggle little less arduous and understand the world better and never feel cheated. Above all it highlights that nothing is really impossible.

—Tarun Kumar Pithode

Part – 1
EARLY LIFE

1

Dewas is a small industrial town situated on Agra – Bombay National Highway. It is surrounded by Ujjain, an ancient Indian city, by Indore, the financial capital of Madhya Pradesh, and Sehore, close to Bhopal, the administrative capital. There is a picturesque hillock right in the heart of the town, which has a serene temple, revered by the people, at its top. Not far away from this hillock there is a Government owned Bank Note Press that prints security paper. Within the secured campus of the Bank Note Press, a small school known as Kendriya Vidyalaya is situated, which are unique institutions as they provide a platform for the convergence of various classes of the society and provide room to interact. It is a school where the children from middle and lower middle class families study, most of whom are government employees. The Bank Note Press is covered from all the sides by high boundary walls, which even the most daring students could not cross. There is a playground where students play football, cricket, hockey, volleyball and variety of other sports.

The school had to raise a football team to participate in regional and national level tournaments and after the autumn break the trials for the selection of new players for filling the vacant positions in the team had started.

"Who wants to take part in the Regional football tournament?" asked the sports teacher in the pre screening session.

Many hands went up hoping that they would get an opportunity to see new places. Considering their fitness and the past records the sports teacher selected twenty-two students and created two teams to play a match that would facilitate the final selection. After four rounds, sixteen players were selected for the tournament.

"All of you have to come for practice till the team leaves for the tournament."

They nodded their heads and said in a chorus, "Yes Sir".

In November the teams were to leave for Patna for interstate regional tournaments. One of the students of IX class, Aditya, who was tall and had athletic body found place in the team and went to play the football tournament. He was full of zestful energy and possessed immense determination to live unto his dreams. As it happens in childhood, young folks hardly know their strengths and their endowments, but he looked forward to an adventurous life.

His father was an accountant in BNP and his mother a housewife. His father had always persuaded him to become somebody in life, but did not know how. His father was a failure in life, for he did not posses the necessary courage to seek out his dreams. His mother, a virtuous lady always narrated to him interesting and instructive stories. He had a younger brother, who was intelligent and from them his parents had great expectations. They had pinned all their hopes on them.

Though a mediocre in the class, Aditya, who shunned hard work, had always aspired to perform well. He had something of an impulsive drive in him that prompted him to try even in the face of defeat. 'What was that?' He could not get an answer.

One day in the class his science teacher asked him to explain photosynthesis. He tried but failed to answer correctly. However, Akash, who was the topper of the class answered, "Photosynthesis is a process of converting light energy from sun into chemical energy by the plants." The teacher appreciated the correct answer.

Not to yield and seek the teacher's attention, Aditya asked, "Madam, if there is no sunlight during the rainy season, why don't the plants die?"

"In the rainy season light does not vanish completely, earth receives diffused light that gets filtered through the clouds and from this meager light, plants make their food and therefore the plants do not die. However, if the sky is filled with such darkness forever, the plants would eventually die", replied the teacher, in a monotonous manner, neglecting the inquisitive zest of the boy, though he had raised a vital scientific issue.

On many occasions, Aditya's inquisitiveness met with cold response. His teachers failed to recognize the validity of his curious questions; nay they failed in their duty to mark that eagerness, which is the first test of intelligence. Asking questions require greater intelligence than answering mugged up answers. Still, he continued to seek their attention, not knowing that teachers, the insensible pedagogues, expect two things from the students, one good performance in the examination and other respect for the teachers. He neither gave an extraordinary performance nor was favourably disposed towards the teachers, for he considered them to be more attentive towards the toppers and the children of influential people. He thought an ideal teacher to be – an advisor, an educator and a guide, who remains free from all biases and considers all the students at par. He was disillusioned with them.

Aditya's struggles to compete and excel against his friends, the family members, who were better off in many ways and the society, unaware of his ambitions, made him uncomfortable. He was not sure of his actions for he had no one with whom to share his feelings and his inner thoughts, which continued to torment him immensely. It was an extraordinary thing for such a small kid to have ego and to aspire for a respectable status. This was mainly due to the joint family in which he lived, where his enhanced sense of self remained unsatisfied. He was a neglected child with less love and more disgust. His parents loved him, though their love was overwhelmed by the expectations of a lower middle class mindset. He became a victim of his parents' expectations, his extended family's disgust and neglect, and his own blotted ego. He wanted to achieve a lot in his life, he was ambitious, yet he did not have a clue, how to achieve his aspirations. If his teachers and his parents had heard the voice of his ego, the situation that pushed him into the worst experiences of his life, at that age, could have been avoided. But, simply none had time to attend to his mortification.

Amid his struggle, he met Rafiq, who was also a part of the football team, and was equally confused about his life. Confusion is the most dangerous thing in the life of an adolescent. Slowly and gradually they came close to each other and found that they loved each other's company, as both of them were directionless despite full of energies. Though, they belonged to different sections of the same class, they frequently met. The participation in the football tournament further strengthened their friendship.

Rafiq was slim with square face and peculiar round eyes. He was a sharp boy with excessive confidence and temerity. He was full of strategies and planning abilities, which remained fictional and never acquired the force of reality. He was an ordinary looking boy, but was capable of performing unimaginable things. His father was a plumber and of his five brothers and three sisters, he was the youngest in the family.

□

2

The day arrived when they had to leave for Patna. They had practiced and were ready to take on their rivals. They met at the bus stand to leave for Itarsi by road to board a train for Patna. One of the teachers accompanied them. Patna was a little more than one thousand and five hundred kilometers away. They reached Itarsi and boarded the train. Though, they had berths to sleep, they preferred to sit on the door of the coach instead, while the train chugged along. It was dangerous, however, nobody stopped them, except their burdensome teacher. Away from their homes they enjoyed the freedom. The teacher escorting them warned, "sitting at the gate could be dangerous and newspapers carry one or the other ghastly story of such accidents when people fall and die, venturing foolishly, at the gate in a running train."

The journey was breathtaking. It was a beautiful sight for these first time travellers. Greenery dominated their journey from Itarsi and beyond, till they crossed the borders of Madhya Pradesh, a thickly forested state.

Once the teacher went for a nap after the lunch, four boys went back to the gate to enjoy the ride. Two each sat on the doors facing each other on either side.

"How beautiful is the route?" commented one.

"I am travelling in train for the first time," revealed the other one.

"Away from home, I am feeling relieved from the pressure of studies and daily routine of the school. How nice it would be if we were to travel forever", said Aditya.

"How much money have you brought?" asked another.

"Why do we need money?" asked Aditya. Others laughed at his innocence.

"You do not know since it is the first time for you. We need money for many things like eating, drinking and smoking", ridiculed the first one at which they laughed even more, while two seniors took out cigarette and started smoking.

"We can't smoke in the train."

They giggled and said, "you should mind your own business."

Aditya kept quiet afterwards. It was dark when the train stopped at a station after running without break for three hours. They took dinner at the station as the train stopped for half an hour. Aditya and Rafiq went to sleep once they had finished the dinner. Others joined them after their routine ablution of smoking.

The train took more than a day to reach Patna in the afternoon. They would stay in a classroom of the school where the accommodation for various teams was arranged. Sixteen teams came from various schools across the region to participate in the tournament. They took rest after finishing lunch and went to a local market as evening engulfed the town, where some of them bought things, while others just strolled.

They got back to find a notice posted adjacent to the door of the classroom. It showed that their match was scheduled in the first round of the tournament the next morning. Not expecting a first match in the tournament the teacher and the captain assembled everybody, hurriedly, and explained them the strategy to be followed in the match, as they were to play against Lucknow, which was famous for a very vigourous defense. Aditya was given the responsibility to play as Centre forward, 'the main striker'. It was a big responsibility. Rafiq was the goalkeeper.

It appeared to be a dull morning when a whistle signalled the start of game for the first half. Sun was shining brilliantly, though, a green field full of grass provided the cushion against the excess perpetrated by the sun. Aditya made some failed attempts at the goal post, but could not do much, as he did not get desired passes from his teammates. He hit three shots at the goal frantically, but none materialized. The other team dominated the game and scored 0-2 increasing their miseries and anxieties. Captain and the teacher guided them and told about the weakness of the opponents during the first half break.

"We played awfully. If Rafiq had not saved two shots on the goal, the score would have been 0-4. Where has the defense gone? I want no more excuses now. We will have to give our best. We are not playing even fifty percent of our capabilities", observed the captain.

"We have a weak midfield," commented the teacher.

"Aditya you will have to play at the center half position rather than forward."

"I will do that."

They finalized the strategy in ten minutes while eating bananas and gulping down lemon juice mixed with glucose. The game of second half started with another whistle. This time the team played with full throttle. If they were to loose this game they would not have any chance of playing in the second stage. Their efforts fructified, ultimately. Aditya scored two goals taking the score to 2-2. There was a late header by the captain, who played as center forward in the second half, leading to their victory over Lucknow with a final score of 3-2.

It was a good day for them. They watched other matches.

Aditya was watching another match when his eyes fell on a girl on the other side of the ground. She came with her friends and sat near them in the second half of the match.

She was intricately woven in curly dark hairs, which was a thing to play for her. So beautiful she was that drove the imagination above the sky and below the depth of an ocean. Though, her beauty was an asset, which might not have lasted for long, but it cast spell on others. Her rectangular hand with long fingers passing through her hairs broke the tranquility of the viewer's mind. To restrain oneself from being a lover was inevitable.

It was operose for an atheist to desist from idol worship – worship the image of this beauty in the temple of his mind. Like a devotee, he too, entered into the sacrosanct rituals of salvation of the youth – eve-watching. The heaven brought on the earth or the earth lifted to the sky was difficult to tell. Her curves were hidden, but noticeably beautiful, needing no further perfection. Yet, the beauty was humble and ignorant of her assets. So easy to access, but so difficult to reach and breach. She was personification of a poet's imagination. God of beauty incarnated. She was Arpita.

He blushed when somebody from among them commented, "You played very well today." He kept on pondering over the possibility of friendship, but could not gather the courage to utter a single word. He watched the match blankly. The last match for that day was over. They looked at each other before she left. Aditya was still looking at infinity while she was gone. Rafiq interrupted him, "the match is over and the audience is gone. Where are you looking now?"

"I was lost somewhere", he said blissfully.

"Shall we go back or you want to extend the rapture, if some is left", said Rafiq giddily. They returned to their place of stay, the school classroom where sixteen of them with their teacher were dumped. The most inconvenient thing was that three teams were to share two common toilets.

They went to the local market in the evening, which was the only place for amusement in that locality.

"Would you like to smoke?" asked Rafiq.

"I have never smoked before," replied Aditya.

"There is always a first time whenever a new person starts smoking."

Aditya tried one puff, but did not like it. He snatched the packet from Rafiq and threw it. Rafiq watched him in disbelief and quizzed, "what are you doing?"

"We should not smoke. It will not only reduce our stamina but kill us as well", cautioned Aditya

The matter ended there. Rafiq took out the extra pack he had purchased and threw it away in a garbage dump. They pledged not to smoke again. It was the beginning of a close friendship between them. The following day they would face Patna. Winning the match would ensure their selection in the National squad. Top teams were to go to Delhi to play National tournaments.

They passed their time, returned and decided to take a stroll around the school campus before they went for dinner. "I am tired and feeling sick. I will go back and sleep", informed Rafiq before leaving for the room.

They took a detour of the school before joining other teams for the dinner. They interacted with the others and learned about various places they had come from. After finishing the dinner when they returned to their dormitory, they were vastly amused at what they saw as soon as the lights were switched on.

"Get up Rafiq!" they screamed while Aditya covered him with a bed sheet.

The tired Rafiq was in such a deep sleep that there was no response. They threw water over him. He woke up and shouted, "What is going on?"

Before he could say anything he realized that he had nothing over his bare body that was wet with water. He froze with shock.

"How the hell are you sleeping?" asked the teacher.

"I do not know anything, Sir. I was tired and sick so I came back and slept instantly. Where are my clothes?"

They looked for his clothes. To their surprise neither his clothes nor his football kit could be traced.

"Some one has played mischief. I will report this matter to the principal of the school", said the teacher after assessing the situation.

"Sir, please keep it a secret otherwise tomorrow they will make fun of us", said the captain.

"We will punish them", exclaimed someone, who was calmed by the sensible teacher, who was busy pondering what must have happened in their absence.

"May be it was done to incite you and ensure your departure tonight itself. Leave the matter, I will handle it in my own way, go and get some sleep. We have to win tomorrow." encouraged the teacher.

While Rafiq was profoundly asleep, a player of Patna team had removed his clothes and poured toothpaste over his bare body with the help of other friends to embarrass him and the team so that they play with vengeance and lose.

* * *

They were full of zeal and energy to win when they assembled on the ground to play against the host Patna. The match started with the sound of a whistle. Referees started to run with all the energies they had. None of the team scored in the first half. The opponents were giving good run to them for the money and energy they had spent in reaching Patna. After the first half the score was 0-0.

When the match for the second half started, Aditya kicked two beautiful shots, but was frustrated by the alertness, focus and concentration of the goalkeeper, who did not allow the ball to enter inside the goal post. He tried another time, while he was dribbling through the defense of the opponent, somebody pushed him and kicked on his toes. For some time he was airborne, clueless as to where and how would he fall? He fell on a rough surface injuring his knee and wrist.

"Son of a bitch! How the hell is he playing", shouted their captain angrily when some players surrounded an injured Aditya, some shouted in anger and some other argued with the referee. Their teacher came and calmed them to stop them from entering into a fight.

The referee was quick to show a yellow card to the boy, who had kicked Aditya. The boy was, however, apologetic and offered his hand to help and lift Aditya, who took it, unwillingly and irritably.

No team scored till the allotted time was over. They got additional four minutes of injury time. Though both the teams played with full vigour and commitment, Dewas looked tired by the end of the match. May be, it was due to smoking and drinking by the senior members of the team, who looked tired and pale and were gasping in the second half of the match. It was the last minute of the game when the opponent goalkeeper kicked the ball, which was collected by one of their players skillfully. He passed it to another one standing before the penalty area with lightning speed. He dribbled and kicked with full strength. Rafiq's eyes were firmly on the ball, despite his repeated lapses into the last night's incident during the game. He jumped to catch it in the direction he anticipated. He was in the air when the ball swung, eluded him and entered into the goal post before he could move his hand in that direction. They wondered in disbelief. How did it happen? Nobody expected a last minute surprise. A long blow of the whistle ended the game. They were outperformed by Patna and the tournament was over for them.

"My name is Brajesh", said the boy, who had kicked Aditya, apologetically, after the match while the girl was looking pathetically at him from a distance. "I am Aditya. Forget what happened on the field", they smiled and parted. She tried to come towards them, but before she could they had already left.

Tired and dejected, they collected their certificates of participation and left the following morning, unceremoniously.

□

3

Rafiq and Sayid were together in tuitions. Sayid had an unusually long neck and his friends called him "camel" with love. He was a charming and handsome boy, who lacked cunningness, which was so typical of Rafiq. His father was a mechanic in the government garage and he was the eldest among his siblings. He too entertained fantasies of living an adventurous life.

Tuition brought Rafiq and Sayid together, whereas, football made Aditya and Rafiq great pals. Sayid and Aditya were in the same section of standard IX and met frequently in the tuition classes. It was a strange combination for all were drifters.

More than the world's disregard, which they faced at different times and places, it was this zeal that had brought them together. After a few months, their regular meetings in school and in tuition brought about a rare proximity. These three boys came together more by fate than the similarity of their trait of wild fantasies, and the dream of living an adventurous life. It is a peculiar feature of young friendships that friends vow to live and die for one other. Adolescence brings many challenges in its wake and these three boys felt its onset. It is the most vulnerable and peculiar period in the life of an individual. A few words of love and demonstration of care can help him to lead a healthy and good life. Their parents were so busy in their lives that they scarcely knew what was happening in the lives of their children and what their ignorance would cost them.

There was something common about these three kids: they all were a product of their schoolteachers, relatives, family friends and above all the ignorance of their parents. Schoolteachers paid attention only to the bright ones, who would someday bring laurels to them and their school. The neglect was so intense that there was hardly any mention of them in any activity. No teacher ever thought of caring for students of their kind. There was nothing that could have stopped these boys from going stray. The neglect and disdain with which the society treated them resulted in a quiet development of contempt and hatred against the society. They were not clear about the means to achieve what they wanted. And this uncertainty filled them with a rebellious spirit against the world and drove them to tread a different path. It forced them to seek revenge against the world.

School is a center of learning both academic and extra-curricular activities. However, due to the lack of attention these boys were alienated and exposed more and more to the indifference and neglect of the society, and more specially due to the lack of love and care of their parents and teachers. They could have been brought into the social fold, but they were alienated through neglect. Good teachers shape the future of the students, but where are they. It is unfortunate that these boys were detached from others and left to themselves to face the harsh realities of life. The first institution of composite socialization had failed them and they in turn were failing the expectations of their parents while the faith of society in these institutions of learning was fast waning.

* * *

The exams for IX standard of the school were over. Aditya, Rafiq and Sayid met regularly away from the gaze of their parents and other friends, none of whom knew what transpired between them.

Aditya was not sure of his results. He was not getting good cues and was beset with lack of confidence. Most of the time he had performed a little better than average in exams and had earned reasonable grades. He knew that he had not given his best this time, particularly when he was not satisfied with his performance. Though he had never topped in the class, he was not sure of maintaining even his previous levels of achievement. For more than studies, he was spending time with his friends away from home – a fact his family was quite unaware.

His anxiety, therefore was apparent on the day result was to be declared. They had passed their exams with second division. It was not an exception for others, but for Aditya, who for the first time missed the first division. He performed short of his expectations, and those of his parents, who were quite unaware of the results.

***

On a fabulous evening, the sky was overcast with clouds, waiting for the arrival of monsoon after a warm summer noon. There was a brief spell of pre monsoon rains that drenched the beautiful breeze blown hillock. Sitting on a cliff Aditya and Rafiq were looking at a blue line curling through at a distant place, while Sayid looked at the blue sky covered with intermittent golden clouds. They frequently came to this place, which was usually calm and provided the right environment to discuss things without any disturbance.

After passing the exams they were discussing their future at the top of the hill. They were pondering over the idea of leaving their homes to do something extraordinary. 'What is that extraordinary thing?' They did not know.

Rafiq was frustrated with the indecisiveness on their part. "We should now leave our homes and take a giant leap to achieve something phenomenal in our lives. We will earn a lot of money and wreck revenge upon the world for people respect money and power", he said with childish anger. Aditya did not expect such a move suddenly, though he was the one to propound this idea first. He thought they would make a perfect plan and then leave. He did not appreciate Rafiq's hurry and desperate action.

"But where will we go? We have no idea and no plans", quipped Aditya.

"Do we still need a plan when we have fire in our hearts? We have already decided to leave and go to Mumbai to start our own business or do whatever is required to become rich", said Rafiq, with a puerile zeal.

"Whatever?"

"Yes, Whatever."

Aditya surrendered to Rafiq's ruthless energy and untested confidence and his own quest to achieve something that fetches respect for him. Rafiq was hell bent to show to the society what youth is capable of. Aditya did not want to lose the precious congenial company he had with these two friends. Sayid was a free radical, who might have gone anywhere; this time he was with them. He had already given his unqualified consent to their decision and whatever they prepared to do, he told them once, "I am with you whatever you do."

How dangerous such drifted youths could be? How important it is to handle children with love and care. It saves lives from getting lost and wasted, a painful truth these boys would learn later, when they would be confronted with the grim realities of the world. Is it not true that many a child could be saved from becoming delinquent, if only teachers and parents treat children with love and care? The energies of the youth could be channelized before they lose direction and are lost to their family and the society.

"Yes, we should decide our destiny", responded Sayid.

Aditya was watching them with great amusement, as if they had won the world.

"Where will we go?" asked Aditya.

"We have a lot many places to go if we have fire in our bellies", Rafiq and Sayid responded together.

"Why not wait for the right opportunity and time?" argued Aditya, trying once again to dissuade them, but his wishes appeared unimportant compared to Rafiq's.

"Don't discourage us by suggesting such dampeners to our enterprise. It was you, who initially shared the idea with us", said Sayid.

Finally, Aditya surrendered. These boys were the victims of ignorant parents, indifferent teachers and the selfish society that hardly cares for the underprivileged and the insignificant. Friendship had provided them succor and saved them from the onslaught of the selfish society for which they had nothing, but hatred.

Rafiq disclosed, unilaterally, "Saturday will be the right day to leave", and they agreed to leave for Mumbai by train. They had seen on Television and in many movies that it was a city of dreams. They were told that people left their homes to go to Mumbai and had made fortunes, not knowing, how many of them had perished in the adventure. To realize their dreams Mumbai was the destination.

□

4

On a mirthful morning, the sky was clear and sun brilliant. Aditya, Rafiq and Sayid met in the morning to confirm that they would set out on their mission in the evening. They decided that they should take permission from their parents for at least two hours of playtime, to ensure they do not panic by their absence, and by the time they discover their absence, it would be difficult to trace them. They parted after confirming once again that they were still together. They were anxious. They trusted each other but exigencies are not bound by trust. It was a day like any other day for people, who had known them, hardly aware of the gathering storm in the minds of these boys.

It was dusk and darkness was setting in, but the stars had not yet studded the sky. People were returning home after the day's hectic work. When Aditya started for the station, he was interrupted by his uncle, "where are you going Aditya?"

"Nowhere uncle, I am going to meet one of my friends."

"Can you bring me a packet of cigarette?"

"Sure uncle, but I will return after two hours."

"Why will it take so long for you? Are you trying to avoid me?"

"No uncle I am going to study at my friend's house."

"But your summer vacations have already begun, what would you study now? Were you studious enough, you would not get such bad grades."

Deeply annoyed by uncle's interrogations and accusations he decided to bring cigarette first and to leave later. He took money, ran and brought cigarette with a lightning speed, handed them to the old man and walked out.

"Now a days children do not respect old people. I asked for a small favour and he started lying", the uncle murmured when Aditya was gone.

It was getting dark yet a reddish splash was visible on the sky between blue and black sky. Rafiq and Sayid had reached the railway station before Aditya and were waiting for him, standing anxiously, at the railway station, with their hearts ponding and their faces drawn. A nagging fear of getting caught gripped them. Besides, Aditya's absence added to their anxiety.

"Where is he?" asked Rafiq.

"I don't know", responded Sayid. And they saw him running towards them.

As decided earlier, they were to leave for Mumbai. They enquired and learned that the train to Mumbai had already left. So they made further enquiries.

"Sir, how can we go to Mumbai?" asked Rafiq.

A tired looking indifferent railway employee at the enquiry counter told them that they could take a train to Indore from where they would get lots of train for Mumbai.

"Let us leave for Indore from where we will take another train for Mumbai", suggested Sayid.

"His duty is to provide service, but he behaves as if he is doing us a favour", said Aditya expressing displeasure at the inquiry man's behaviour.

"Do not bother such things keep on happening", replied Rafiq.

"What is inside this bag?"

"You forget so easily dear", said Rafiq, he smirked and continued, "These are our weapons."

"I am impressed", said Sayid, "that you remembered to bring these things, they will be very useful to us", he continued while Aditya froze.

"What if somebody asks us why are we at the station and where are we going, what would we say?" asked a worrying Aditya.

"You bother too much Aditya", responded Rafiq, impervious to reason.

Sayid did not say anything; he knew that he would get a similar reply, though, until Aditya arrived it was Rafiq, who was bothering.

"Why is the train taking so long in coming? Why is it late today?" an anxious and agitated Aditya asked again.

"I am telling you, if you are so restive, things would be difficult." There was sound of a coming train, which was increasing constantly, and that reduced the unease on the countenances of these adolescents. They looked at each other and smiled wryly.

"Rafiq, we will take on either the last or the first compartment", cautioned Sayid, fearfully.

"Second or Second last would be equally good", said Aditya.

"We will board the first compartment that stops in front of us. We have left home and let us leave the homely worries home, said Rafiq.

"Are we doing the right thing by running away from home without even telling our parents. They will search us for the whole night, should we write a letter telling them that we are leaving", suggested Sayid, remorsefully.

"Once we have decided to leave, now we can't look back. We have taken a decision, right or wrong, it should not change. Do you think that telling them will help? It will rather complicate the situation. There is no need to inform anybody. They will know it sooner or later", said Rafiq putting all doubts to rest.

"But they might fear that we have been kidnapped", Aditya said in a worrying voice.

"Whatever they might feel let them. If we have to achieve something, we will have to be strong in life", said Rafiq fretting at their worries.

They were all silent and preferred not to speak about home.

The train arrived raucously and they boarded the second last compartment that stopped before them. After a brief halt, the Guard in the last compartment whistled and waved the flag, and the train started speeding up. They took a sigh of relief realizing that no one had seen them leaving the town. None of them had ever left the town alone. These delinquents assumed that they had all the strength and cunningness to conquer the world. In their felicity and elation, they forgot to buy tickets.

"I feel I am free now and I can show to the world that I do not care for it and I too can be powerful and rich", said Aditya. He was angry towards the society that never gave him importance, especially within his extended family of rich and influential people.

As the train started, they took seats near the window. A cool breeze that entered the compartment signaled that monsoon was knocking at the door. Indian monsoon brings great relief after the agony of hot and humid months from April to June. The rising sun could never have apprehended that it would be fully concealed by the clouds to stop spreading its beauty in the horizon. Clouds had their own plans to make the evening a joint venture.

Downfalls may be many, though some are unique. Some degeneracy imparts people a learning experience to escape them. People hardly feel that they fail because of their own weakness and not because fate has conspired against them. People always blame others for their failures and shortcomings. Aditya thought that his two friends could do anything for him. Often, such a stupid self-assurance can be the beginning of a tragic decadence. Collectivism combined with loss of objective thinking always lead to decline. They were so zestful that nothing could have stopped them.

A dark man, who looked drunk, sat in front of them. His belly ominously bulged, as if to come out of his shirt; his mouth was plump and eyes dark red.

"Where are you going?" asked the dark man politely – a politeness, which was more discomforting than assuring.

They were annoyed with the query, for he demanded a reply. But Rafiq kept his cool and answered, "We are going to Indore. Our uncle will come to receive us."

"Where do you want to go there? Will you all go to the same place in Indore? Are you all relatives?"

"We want to go to Vijay Nagar, our uncle will come to receive us, and we are cousins."

"I have hardly seen children of your age travel alone."

"We are quite grown up now."

"Which class do you study in?"

"We have passed IX standard and are fourteen years of age."

"What is your name", the dark man suddenly asked Aditya.

Bewildered by the question, he replied nervously and deceitfully, "I am Anis Khan", while Rafiq and Sayid looked at him with surprise and disbelief, his voice hushed.

"And you?"

"I am Rafiq and he is Sayid", replied Rafiq, trying to cut short the interrogations.

Aditya's heart was pounding against the ribs heavily thinking what they would do if someone asked for the ticket. He was wearing respectable clothes and a watch. What a great beginning for his teens!

The train passed through a lovely meandering route; soon, it became dark and nothing was visible, except the twinkling fireflies. Cold breeze was entering inside the general compartment of the train through open windows. They were entranced by the journey, until the vernal air entering the window of the train appeared bitter and sultry, as someone squatting in the next cubical was smoking cigarette, unscrupulously, polluting the air inside. Nearby, some people were fighting over seats, "I captured it first", said one person, the other claimed to have occupied it before.

Some people were playing cards. It is one of the most popular games and universally practiced pass time in the trains. Two children were selling tea and snacks. Roasted gram is one of the favorite snacks of common people travelling in general class in Indian Railways. These sellers travel without ticket and nobody stops them for they provide services to passengers without service charge. India has legislated against child labour and the RTE expect these children to go to school, but it remains on paper making the ground reality different from the rosy legislations. Implementers do not wish to confront this reality and feel contented with noble laws, but are oblivious to the harsh realities.

"Hey Chotu come here", called the dark man and ordered, "Give me one cup of gram. Mix it properly with spices and sprinkle some lemon juice over it."

He took Gram and started eating while reading a weekly magazine.

"Unkil ten rupees", requested Chotu.

"Sorry I forgot to give."

"If I forget to take the money then I will die." Chotu commented, sarcastically.

The man took out his wallet and handed over a ten-rupee currency note. Rafiq stole a glance and saw that his wallet was full of five hundred rupee currency notes and some change. He had never seen so much money, and felt like snatching it.

□

5

It was completely dark when the train was slowing down. The frequency of whistle was increasing indicating that the station was approaching. Amidst the tension of being caught, they reached their first destination, Indore, after enjoying a free ride, when the train came to a screeching halt. They rejoiced, for nobody asked them for tickets. They got down to take another train to reach Mumbai from another platform.

"We have forgotten our most important bag inside the train", Rafiq informed others after walking for a while. All of them rushed back towards the train and were lucky to retrieve it; they reached and grabbed it as if they had found some treasure. They would know only later if it were fortunate or otherwise.

It was an old grubby school bag full of filth, which looked normal, but contained the most unexpected baggage. There was a sword, a bogus revolver, a knotted rope and a torch indicative of nothing except that these teenagers were playing adulthood. Rafiq brought the sword and bogus revolver that he had bought during last Diwali for fun; the very look of the revolver enthralled him and forced him to buy it. While buying it, he scarcely knew the use he would put to. The sword was not sharp, but was enough to threaten someone with. Aditya brought a small torch, while Sayid brought a rope from his home. His father had bought the rope for supporting the hammock for his youngest cousin;

he had stolen it envisaging they might need it. In anticipation he had knotted the rope, tied and kept it inside the bag. The bag was nothing less than arms and ammunition to these soldiers of destiny. It was the embodiment of a shared effort and shared purpose.

"Hey, boys show your tickets", someone interjected from behind when the elated boys were rejoicing their newly acquired freedom and were about to leave. They turned back only to find the train ticket examiner (TTE). He was tall and plump. He wore a black coat that was flapping against a slow moving rusted fan hanging, wearily.

"Why?"

"I saw you getting down from train, do you still need some more reasons?"

"We do not have tickets", replied Aditya, defensively sensing his mood.

"You scoundrels, I see many like you everyday. Follow me to the cabin", he ordered, with a dreadful voice, sending a wave of shock and despair among the boys, hitherto untouched with the reality of the life. The elation was swallowed by the heavy sardonic voice.

"We do not have tickets. Please sir! Allow us to leave. We have to attend an important function", they pleaded, almost on their knees.

"Checking tickets is my job not hearing excuses."

After confirming that the boys did not have tickets, he incarcerated them in a room and held them captive. One hour passed without anyone caring for them leave alone freeing them. They tried to call people for help, every time someone seemed to have heard them, it was the TTE, who came back to show his exasperation to them.

"I have twenty five rupees, may be this would move this avaricious official", murmured Aditya. They confabulated and concluded that they should handover twenty-five rupees to get out of the tight spot, but the indifferent TTE did not even care to spare them for money. This is typical of corruption in India that people do not even leave a penny when they have a chance to earn through unfair means. May be, it is human nature to exploit the weak.

When the TTE came after half an hour they were already envisioning their fate. "Please leave us. We have not done anything wrong."

"Travelling without ticket is a punishable crime and you have broken the law", said the TTE, glancing them from near making them realize that he was stoned. They, however, neither had the knowledge, nor the courage to tell him that it was rather crime to be inebriated on duty.

"Is there any way we could be spared?"

"You will have to pay the fine. There is no other option."

"How much?"

"You will have to pay fifty rupees; else you all will go to jail."

"We do not have that much money."

"Then go to jail", warned the TTE, prompting tears of indignation.

"I have only twenty five rupees, please take and leave us", said Aditya, as if begging desperately, whose worries at the prospect of going to jail drove him to make a move.

Rafiq was upset with Aditya, but preferred to remain silent. The TTE left the room expressing deep disgust and anger. Experience has its own advantages and these boys did not know that they could not be jailed.

"Give me all the money you have", he said after he came back for the second time after half an hour, being sure that he could not get more than what they had offered.

"Take this we have only this much", Aditya handed him twenty-five rupees with both the hands as if performing a ritual short of prostration.

His cupidity was evident, so was his selfishness and cruelty, when he grabbed it and released them after the bribe was paid as ransom. In this country one can get anything done speedily, after spending money on payola.

"Do not come back again or I will send you to jail", warned the discontented TTE.

He had an unknown fear, which drove him to issue the admonition. They were startled, yet nodded in agreement and left like beaten dogs.

"A loathsome insatiable bastard", murmured Rafiq with stifled anger.

Being emancipated, they came out of the station, loathing and cursing the TTE after the ordeal, discussing about the future course of action with their limited experiences to guide or misguide them; they were dejected and demoralized.

* * *

It was dark and somber outside. They decided to proceed for Mumbai, not by train, but by road now. They saw a cycle-rickshaw puller standing at the outer gate of the railway station smoking bidi, creating a haze of smoke and a fog of ignorance – ignorance of his hunger. Sayid beckoned the rickshaw puller, while Aditya and Rafiq gazed each other with doubt and uncertainty in their minds.

The rickshaw puller was a thin emaciated man with a sinking belly, indicating poverty. He was dark skinned and was wearing a long shirt and loincloth. He moved sighting a hand waving. He took the last puff as if taking the last morsel. Poor men smoke to avoid food; they do not want to avoid it, but do not have enough to eat. He dropped bidi, crushed it like a professional smoker and started towards the potential customers not knowing that the potential customers would be indigent like him.

"At this time if somebody is pulling rickshaw that means he is really impoverished", said Sayid, remorsefully; others did not respond.

"Where do you want to go?" asked the rickshaw puller, breathlessly.

"A-B Road", responded Sayid, who had known this city slightly.

"I will take fifty rupees", informed the rickshaw puller, coughing with chocked throat and shrill voice.

Sayid nodded with confidence as if he had money to pay it several times. How does it matter to a penniless, who knows that he has nothing to pay and he could even promise a moon.

"Why are you boys travelling alone at this time? The times are not good, people run away with children and force them to beg in Mumbai", said the rickshaw puller sending shockwaves through their minds.

"We are going to our relative's home", replied Rafiq. The rickshaw-puller thought, "If that was right why would they not tell some specific address"; he shrugged the question and dismissed the thought.

"Have you come from outside?"

"Yes."

"I will tell your relative not to send you at this time if I meet them, the town is real bad."

They travelled for about two kilometers, and tried to hide themselves from the streetlights as if they were robbers under chase. After smelling some danger Rafiq said, "Please stop. We want to get down here", while Sayid and Aditya looked at his interjection surprisingly.

"But you wanted to go to A-B Road."

"We want to get down here now. Please stop."

He stopped and demanded, "ten rupees". They looked at each other then Aditya glanced at rickshaw puller with a sense of guilt and struggled to speak with a choking voice, "We do not have money".

"What?" exploded the thunderstruck rickshaw puller.

"We do not have money", repeated Aditya after regaining his confidence, while others remained silent.

"Then why have you taken my services, please do not play tricks with me. I am penniless and I have nothing to feed my family", said the visibly shocked Rickshaw puller.

Before an argument could break among them, Aditya took out the torch from the bag and said, "you may take it we do not have a single penny, we have lost our money while travelling in the train – we are not lying". The genuineness with which Aditya had put his request, the Rickshaw puller readily agreed to accept the offered compensation. It was meaningless to face three young well-fed boys at the outskirts of the city alone. They asked for the route to reach A-B road. He spoke with fear, showed the way and left never looking back.

Nevertheless, he reconciled with the reality, and was contented that his wife would feel glad, who had been demanding a torch from him since ages. In many parts of the country the poor people go some distance away from their houses to defecate, especially, women, who prefer to go in the dark so that they are not exposed to public shame. "This torch would help her", he thought.

When the Rickshaw-puller gradually disappeared in the streetlights, guilt seized their conscience, for they had deprived honest wages to a poor man. The poor man, who lived on smoke had nothing to eat tonight. They were genuinely sad. They had already handed over, whatever they had, to the Train Ticket Examiner. Their dream of splendor encountered a harsh reality.

□

6

Aspirations, howsoever bad, may generate enough fire in the hearts of the people to find solutions to their worst problems. Their predicament forced them to walk. They crossed the city. Three silhouettes were clear, when they were walking in the background of the beautiful sparkling lights, far away from them now. There was a stretch of forest before they reached near any habitation. After walking considerable distance, when they reached near a dhaba, the appetizing scent of the food made them feel famished. On reaching near, they peeped inside, eagerly, and saw people eating and drinking. The sight and the fact that they were penniless further sharpened their hunger. Looking at the trucks parked nearby, Rafiq thought of taking lift from them to reach Mumbai.

"Let us try getting lift from the drivers of these trucks. Someone may take us to our destination", said Rafiq and prodded them.

"Why should they take us for free?" enquired Sayid.

"I am not sure, though we are not left with any other option but to try and walk", replied Rafiq.

"I am feeling like eating a horse and it will take ages to reach Mumbai on foot", said Sayid.

"We may forget food for a while, for being without money we should not indulge in any further stupidity that would lead us to clean the utensils and detain us here till the next morning. So it is better to try hitchhiking", expressed Aditya. All agreed.

They tried with five vehicles, but failed and finally chose to walk. Aditya now maintained some distance by remaining behind Rafiq and Sayid. While walking he tried two times and succeeded in getting a truck stop. Sayid and Rafiq were little ahead as part of the strategy to get the lift. They came running towards Aditya as the truck stopped. They were luckily taken on board.

"Where are you guys going alone so late in the night?" asked the driver.

"We are going back to our home in Mumbai, we missed the last train and we are left with no money so we are trying to take lift. We have to reach our homes as soon as possible", replied Sayid.

The driver did not trust them. However, thinking that they might be child labour, he did not make any further inquiry.

"Despite many efforts, the problem of child labour persists", he thought.

"But I am going in another direction. I am going towards Pithampur", revealed the driver and asked, "Do you guys want to continue?"

"No", replied Rafiq.

They got down and continued walking. The night was getting darker with the passage of time. In the presence of thick black clouds, full of lightening thunder, the dark night grew darker with intermittent burst of lightening. These clouds were diffracting the light they absorbed from a distant place, blissfully giving a divine view. Nature was at its best. The view was splendid, but the time and place were hardly encouraging. Left with no other option to fallback on, they continued walking.

Rafiq pointed towards another dhaba. They peeped inside, and found people drinking, chatting, eating and even quarrelling.

Sayid observed, "This is not the right place to wait".

"Yes", nodded Aditya and Rafiq.

They had hardly walked some distance when the clouds pregnant with water began to pour suddenly and heavily. They had no place to hide, and they were completely drenched.

"There is no shelter nearby, let's take shelter under some tree", advised Rafiq.

"We should never stand under a tree as during rains lightning strikes such shelters," they looked in disbelief while Aditya continued, "I have studied science." He could not hide his common sense and general knowledge.

After it poured heavily, drenched Aditya let his emotions loose, he opened himself for the first time after leaving the home. "Enough is enough", he thought. He doffed his shirt off, while Rafiq and Sayid watched, astonishingly. They were surprised by the ease with which he seemed to have forgotten everything. He exploded, "I am on cloud number nine."

"You stopped us from going under the tree to save ourselves from lightning, but now you are exposing yourself to the source of that lightning, may God help you", commented Sayid at which they laughed.

It lightened the heaviness they experienced after they boarded the train to leave their homes, were caught by the TTE and were overburdened with the guilt arising from non-payment to the rickshaw puller. Nonetheless, they themselves did not know how short-lived such thoughts could be.

"How long we should walk and where should we stop?" asked Sayid.

Nobody replied as none of them had any clue, though they could see some dull and tired light emanating from a village, which was a little ahead; they moved towards the source of the light, which was not far away now.

* * *

The road wore a deserted look until they crossed a village named Bhatkhedi on A-B road. When they crossed a dhaba in which some people were eating, some were smoking and playing carom board and some others were drinking in that odd hour of the night, Aditya's watch struck 12, with both the hands merged together, as if they were greeting their arrival; they continued to walk for another half a kilometer.

A strange thing happened as they decided to return back, an incongruous move that would prove costly to them and soon they would regret it; they were directionless and tired. As they walked past the dhaba again, a man smoking Bidi noticed their return. It was so unusual at this hour of night for kids to stroll on the deserted National Highway. He watched for a brief while to reassure that they were the same boys and then challenged them – "Hey, Who are you?"

"From where are you coming at this time of the night?" the second voice questioned.

"Come here", ordered the third one. They shivered with nervousness, were speechless hearing the dreadful voices, and looked at each other and thought of running away, but sanity prevailed upon them.

"Let us run and get away from this place as soon as possible", said Sayid quivering with fear.

"No, it would be insane to run now", said Aditya,

"They can catch us any moment. They will not spare us if we tried to run away", warned Rafiq.

"Rafiq is right they can catch us easily and they would kill us if we tried to run away, let us surrender to them", suggested Aditya.

Rafiq and Sayid readily agreed. These lads did not know what future awaited them on that dark night. The night was getting darker for them. Soon they were surrounded by a bevy of enigmatic villagers.

The man who howled had a distinguishing, long, dark, ugly and repulsive face with a big mouth like that of hippopotamus. He had a scar on his face that made him appear more frightful than his other companions. His name was Kallu and he owned the shop adjacent to the dhaba.

"Bhai Rajesh, do you know who these guys are? Please see", asked the dangerous looking, Kallu.

Rajesh was a short and dark man with a broad head, flabby cheeks and a short chin. He was wrathful. With a threatening calculative aggression he asked, "Who are you? What the hell are you doing here at this time of the night? Do you belong to this village? I have not seen you here before."

When they came close to him, it was clear that he was dead drunk. They apprehended a physical assault, though only God knew what was in store for them. They encountered the worst cruelty a man is capable of inflicting.

"I have a hunch that these boys are thieves. Now we know where our animals are disappearing for the past one month. Chacha told me that regular thefts are taking place in our village", said Rajesh. The mention of word 'thief' sent a shudder through their spines.

"Yes, Bachchu uncle also told me that his goats were vanishing mysteriously", confirmed Kallu.

"It seems we have caught the culprits", said Rajesh, triumphantly.

"Let us beat them; insert a big rod in their mouth, to be sure they will come out with the truth", cried Kallu, "should we not call Pandu constable, who specializes in extracting truth from such criminals."

"Everyone come here, interrogate them before we thrash them."

The aggressive villagers surrounded the boys. For the boys it was another real encounter and confrontation with the harsh reality of the world where you break your shins. It did not require much effort for them to discover the verity. The boys were terrified. They turned pale with fear. Soon there was a resonating sound of slaps that left the boys red faced. The stoned men shouted obscenities and thrashed the boys mercilessly. Nobody came to rescue the howling and sobbing of runaways.

Kallu with his coterie now interrogated Rafiq and Sayid separately, while Rajesh tortured Aditya. They hardly had anything to hide. Rafiq and Sayid accepted the truth, told them their real names and revealed their intensions of leaving their homes. They told that they had run away from home to seek adventure, earn handsome money and live like lords.

A big slap came on Aditya's face from Rajesh. "Tell us your name", he asked, murderously.

"Anis Khan", replied Aditya, reflexively, with a paralyzed voice subdued by the brutality.

"I cannot trust you, you do not look a Muslim."

Now the room was filled with the sound of sobbing and crying. Aditya was weeping while Rajesh was searching his pockets. The dangerous looking man with stinted eyes and cigarette in his mouth shouted at him, frisked him and found a watch in his pocket. It was a watch – his father had gifted him; he felt apologetic for his father, who loved him so much.

Rajesh questioned, menacingly, "From where did you get this watch? To be sure you have stolen it." He continued, "I do not trust this boy. He is not a Muslim; if removed his pants we would discover the reality", assuming that circumcision is one thing that distinguishes a Muslim from a Hindu. Believing that the boy was from a good family, he roared, "Look I was right this kid is hiding the truth, he must be from a good family as he is wearing a watch, has donned respectable clothes and above all innocent soft looks". He stared at Aditya, ominously, as if to warn him of dire consequences, if concealed his true identity. The special interest with which Rajesh treated him bothered Aditya of some unseen and unexpected outcome, leading him to grovel.

"We cannot trust Muslims as they have taken away Pakistan from us. They deserve to be beaten to death", declared Rajesh with all the vengeance and venom against Muslims.

What he said about Muslims was nothing new, for it was an oft-repeated chagrin and the prejudices still prevailing against them in India. Muslims, who now are a religious minority, were once the rulers of this vast country. Things changed for them after partition that resulted in the creation of Pakistan as an Islamic state. Muslims were not subjected to direct discrimination, but suffered neglect by the majority and problems of their own creation. While other communities and other minorities grew, the largest minority remained under the shackles of poverty and bane of ignorance. It further degenerated due to the lack of modern education and employment. The lack of chances to move ahead led to criminalization and involvement in illegal activities in response to the efforts of subjugation. An average Muslim is not different in looks from other Indians, which indicate that they come of the same genetic stock as any other Indian. However, due to their separate identity, they could not be subjugated the way some other groups, particularly Tribal and Dalit, were subjugated, forcefully, for long time.

Tribal and Dalit for long have been at the receiving end even after independence. They had accepted the subjugation and internalized it. However, they progressed after freedom from British Raj due to the positive discrimination by the state. On the other hand, Muslims lagged, in using the opportunities that freedom from British rule gave, to match other communities in terms of development. It is a tragedy of sorts that Muslim leadership could not be evolved; religious and political leaderships never considered economic and social prosperity of Muslims vital.

Aditya wept and feared that it would be a great disaster if they came to know about his real identity. He insisted on a Muslim name to win their curiosity. The name "Anis Khan" was consistent with two other Muslim friends, so people did not inquire further and trusted him. It also saved his family that enjoyed a good reputation in his locality. Before the second round of interrogation began, Rafiq requested to call his friend Arjun, who had gone to visit his maternal uncle living in that village, a fact, incidentally, known to Rafiq.

Meanwhile Rajesh opened the bag –a can of worms for the boys, which was an invitation to another disaster, while the boys watched his moves, anxiously; while Arjun was called, the boys were beaten again to explain the circumstances and truth behind its content, especially, the sword, fake revolver and rope discovered by Rajesh, who took out the rope and showed it to everybody justifying the possibility expressed by Chacha and Bachchu uncle.

"Look what I told you, is true, for tonight these kids had come for committing theft in our village", Rajesh spoke with reassurance.

"Yes, we have run away from home", interrupted Aditya with a choking voice, whose patience had run out of steam, "but it is equally true that we have never committed any crime or offence, though we have left our homes chasing our dreams", continued Aditya quivering with fear, and he was stammering.

"We wanted to become rich and powerful so we resolved to leave home and run away to a dreamland to realize our dreams. It is the first time we have come out from home. We kept these things for our safety and not for any offence or crime", a trembling Sayid tried to explain. Aditya nodded while Rafiq remained dumb and looked away pale with fear. Rafiq was unapologetic for he possessed the traits of a prospective hardened criminal.

Tears in their eyes, finally yielded some results, as those thugs seemed receptive to the argument that these boys were not habitual offenders and they were doing it for the first time, they would not be caught were they professional dacoits or thieves. They would have not returned seeing so many rustic men sitting at that hour of the night in their savage wilderness. Their age was corroborating the submissions, arguments and confessions, they made.

It was an age of revolt in which they believed that people could become rich and powerful by running away from home. They were not maltreated at home, but were neglected. They did not receive the attention they deserved in the society, and beyond the imagination of a common man, running away was the manifestation of the lack of adventure in their life, which neither their home nor the school could provide.

Instinctively, human being is born free and is ready to face any eventuality to defend it; one lives to express it, often, unknowingly; every act of him if analyzed deeply, reveals only one truth – the freedom of expression. The expression of this freedom can happen in the best forms of art, culture, religion, socialization or any other act. Yet he becomes prisoner of his own freedom donned by the burden of ignorance; the boys were driven by that very instinct, but a little before their age and time, and more than a little towards the extreme.

* * *

At that hour of the night, Arjun arrived shaken and shocked. The person who was sent to identify him revealed everything on the way. "Here is Arjun, now the truth shall come out", said Kallu while Arjun entered the room.

"Yes, I know him", told Arjun looking despondently at Rafiq whose face was swollen due to the beatings he had received. He knew these thugs very well. The boys took a sigh of relief once their identity was acknowledged among the ruffians.

"What if these hooligans tell everything to Arjun, and what if he discloses everything to our parents? What will happen to the pride of my father, he would be devastated if he comes to know of this disgraceful incident", thought Aditya, which cluttered his mind.

After Arjun's recognition of Rafiq's identity, the temperatures, which were running high before Arjun's entry, came down. They had to decide the future of these boys and their return to home; they pondered over whether to hand them over to police or surrender them to their parents. The boys did not know what transpired between them after they were pushed back in the backyard to eat, while those delighted villagers babbled. Despite being hungry, not even a single morsel could go down their throats.

On the other side those who were playing carom board started again; those who were smoking lighted another bidi; and those who were eating started asking for warm chapattis, as if nothing had happened in the last one hour. It was business as usual, and there was nothing new about the recent episode except that it involved adolescents. They relished each bit of it, hedonistically.

"Let us send them to the city after seizing their material so that they could go back from there to their respective homes", proposed Rajesh pitying their state.

"Motu will shortly leave for Indore to sell his grains in Mandi and he will drop them there", decreed Rajesh, the owner of the dhaba, and a self styled leader of these night watchmen. They all respected him because of his influence on the nightlife of this small village that provided an avenue for entertainment to the rural folks, otherwise devoid of entertainment. They agreed to send the boys to the city and communicated their plan to them, not telling them the proposed handover. "They will be taken to the city by Motu's tractor and will be delivered to the police there", pronounced Kallu as if ordering conviction after a long trial taking a jeer at them. While he said this, the boys were not sure of their fate, though, when Arjun intervened, they were assured that they would only go back to their homes and not to the police station.

The arrival of tractors at this unusual time at late night was a usual incidence in the village. Before leaving for the Mandi, farmers used to take tea, chat and chew pan or smoke bidi and get the latest news about the village. They always left late at night to ensure their place in auction.

Motu was a farmer cum grain trader, who arrived there with loads of grain to be sold in the Mandi. He greeted everybody and ordered tea. He was surprised to find boys there, at that moment. He enquired about them and was apprised of the happenings during the past one-hour. He was not drunk and was sympathetic to them as he fathered two sons and two daughters of the same age.

"Let us not threaten them anymore, I will drop them in the city at a convenient place from where they can leave for their home", said Motu with mercifulness.

They were almost beaten to death, and experienced the worst horror of their lives; they were deeply terrified by the incident. There was a haze of fear in the air. It was a nightmare they would never want to happen again, not even to their enemies. They were ashamed and there was a sense of guilt in their heart, especially, Aditya and Sayid, who had never encountered such humiliation before. They had faced neglect, but not disrespect that made them feel insulted, humiliated and dishonoured. They never imagined that they would be punished so harshly for a small mistake, nevertheless their good luck had saved them from a genuine tragedy.

□

7

The last one-hour seemed like an era to them. They rode on top of the heap of grain bags in the tractor trolley, nonchalantly, and the tractor left for the city. Still they had a lurking fear in their mind, for they were not habitual offenders and scarcely knew the crime world. Many a time they were beaten at homes for small lapses, but never experienced the kind of horror they faced recently. They were under great mental stress, but as they passed by the police station they were sure that they were Mandi bound.

If fact, when the tractor stopped at a place where the little patch of jungle ended, just before entering the city, Aditya asked Rafiq," should we run away?" while they were urinating against a tree along with Motu and others. It is a common sight in India in the absence of public toilets.

"No", replied Rafiq, emphatically, and the matter ended there. They returned back to take their respective places in the trolley.

"How strange is it that we just crossed a jungle which might be full of wild animals", said Aditya sadly, speaking freely after a long time when they got on to the tractor.

"What do you want to say", asked Sayid, puzzled at Aditya's bizarre observation.

"A Jungle is full of variety of animals, carnivorous, omnivorous and herbivorous. Similarly, we have people in our society; some are carnivorous, some like omnivorous and others like herbivorous."

"You seem to have lost your mind", said Sayid.

"No, I have not. The animals which we encountered in the past six hours explain everything about the idea I shared."

"Animals! How?" asked Sayid, astonishingly.

"We tumbled into the hands of a TTE, who was like a carnivore. He did not care about our innocence and age before extracting bribe from us. He was concerned only about money and he had no humanity and sensitivity. He would treat influential and powerful people with respect and poor and weak with contempt, but would bite, eat and swallow, whenever got an opportunity. He would lick above and kick below."

"What about the rickshaw puller?" asked Sayid, and Rafiq ignored them.

"The rickshaw puller was like a herbivore, who could not do any wrong to anyone. We cheated him for a ride, did not pay him the money he deserved, instead we offered him a torch. He accepted it, as he did not have the capability to attack us or coerce us to give money."

"Is the last category of omnivores?"

"Yes, these were those guys who were sitting in the 'dhaba' at this odd time of the night, as if waiting for a prey. They behaved like carnivores when they caught us, had beaten us and treated us with such crass contempt. However, when it became apparent that we were not as bad as they thought initially, they treated us with kindness and sent us home."

"Impressive analogy Aditya, I appreciate your spirit. Adversity can prompt you to contemplate", commented Rafiq.

"The whole world is like that. We are not human beings but animals. We behave and respond as per the circumstances."

"What about us?"

"Omnivorous."

Now Rafiq and Sayid neglected him and he stopped speaking. The tractor crossed the place where they were dropped by the rickshaw puller not so long ago.

"What a coincidence! It was the same place where the rickshaw puller had dropped us yesterday night. We were high-spirited to begin with, but only four hours later now we are regretful", thought Sayid. They were back to square number two; it was like a nightmare for them. They finally reached Mandi, where Motu dropped them with a caveat to go back to their homes; they nodded gratefully.

"If you fail to reach your homes we would lodge a complaint with police", he warned and left.

* * *

If they thought their dreadful experience ended there, they were mistaken. It was 2:30 am and they saw everybody sleeping covered with short soiled bed sheets on the muddy platforms of the Mandi. A face popped out, through a hole in the bed sheet, to know the reason of disturbance at that unusual time and got back without excitement. They were badly tired and searched for a place to sleep, though they had nothing to cover themselves with, on that cold rainy night. They looked at the rural folks fast asleep with contentment despite the little they had.

Aditya thought, "Should I snatch a bed sheet from someone? No, I cannot stoop to that level!" While they moved from one place to another edging modestly through the crowd, people looked at them with suspicion and disdain. Left with no other option they stayed in the Mandi for the remainder night.

Cold and mosquitoes made life difficult. Filth and stench of the rotten grain, vegetables and cow dung compounded their difficulty. Between slumber and sudden awakening among the smelling jute bags, they somehow passed the remaining night full of drowsiness.

While they sat they saw a shabbily attired, bald-headed old man, still awake, lost in his own dreams or in the problems of daily existence so disturbing among the poor. But poverty and sufferings, nay the poor, are soon forgotten.

The old man was standing in front of the place, these miserable boys had chosen for comforting themselves. Aditya was badly tired, as he was still awake – an unusual thing for him, thus he could hardly notice the old man in details, until the old man spoke, disturbing the serene tranquility engulfing the corner they had chosen to hide and comfort. They learned that this old man lived in the Mandi as his family had deserted him. He loved young men, for in them he found his grandson to whom he was lovingly attached. Poverty or miseries do not affect old age as do loss of love and neglect.

A young man, Kalyan, who had come back from Gwalior to his village to help his father to sell wheat in the Mandi, was standing near the old man, who was in high spirits and questioned the young man.

Aditya and others were sitting at a small distance away, now pored over the old man in conversation with Kalyan, who was all ears.

"When did you come here son?"

"I came last week to Indore and then to my village. "

"What are you doing now? "

"I have joined a government job as a junior engineer."

The garrulous old man further enquired, "Son how much are you earning?" and before he could give a reply, he continued in anticipation, "You must be earning fifty thousand."

The gentleman already frustrated with the realities of government job, could not remain cool and replied annoyingly, "Don't ask that again, my fine old man, don't you know government servants are offered practically nothing in this country. Higher pay is for higher people". However, he regained his mental balance and good sense and replied, "I earn thirty thousand rupees." The deeply hurt old man, who felt humiliated for Kalyan's curt reply and thought his manner unacceptable, was relieved. He now felt elated by his achievement and retorted without leaving the decency of his manners, "So I am a big man now, grandfather to an officer."

The boy, who was irritated once again, explained angrily, "Dada engineers are not called officers". The behaviour of Indian society remains shamelessly hierarchical, like the old man, who did not feel any shame in assuming the achievement of his grandson to assure himself of his heightened sense of self and a high status of being the producer of a high repute scion.

Kalyan was like any other ordinary man. Though, he was perceptively distinct with his small eyes and a peculiar nose, yet big enough to disqualify being a mongoloid. He feared mongoloids as he thought all of them to be Chinese, who invaded India and left deep scar on the national psyche. They raped, killed, imputed many, looted property and confidence of the people of the Northeast, who hated Nehru for a delayed decision to deploy the army and the air force to attack and reinforce the ground forces.

Kalyan, with lots of aspirations and promises of a better future had joined the government job. It gave him enough space to boast of his singular success, which he did not expect.

Aditya and his friends, watching these two men deeply lost in conversation, tried to forget the muddle of the past few hours, and pulled themselves out of the depth of the slur they experienced. The old man obsessed with his past and a young one obsessed with his future.

□

8

It was six in the morning. A delightful dawn gave them some energy and comfort to recuperate from the horrible experience they had undergone. Every comfort is the beginning of a new discomfort and challenge. They realized that they had expected too much from themselves in this cruel social environment to achieve something uncommon to their age. They were wrong to assume that money could be easily earned through any objectionable means including theft and robbery.

After they had exhausted all their resources, particularly, the determination and courage to become rich in a free country, they decided to go back to the railway station to catch a train back to Dewas. They left for the railway station with the hope that once again they would be free to take a ride on the train.

They arrived at the railway station and were happy to notice that the train was being shunted at the platform for the passengers to board. They passed time by sauntering about the length of the platform to escape the gaze of the railway officials. Their difficulty did not end there when the Murphy's Law – 'anything that can go wrong will go wrong' proved right. They were dumbstruck to see the same TTE, who had hooked them the previous night coming towards them along with the Station Master; he did not fail to identify them.

"What the hell are you doing here? Do not even dare to think for a moment to get into the train, otherwise you would be in jail", said the TTE. They could not understand the reason of such contempt. However, the venom with which TTE scolded them forced them to leave the station, depressed and humiliated. They thought of boarding the train at the level crossing, but chose to abandon the misadventure; they rather preferred to walk to Dewas, nonchalantly.

"Had we been in Dewas, we would have taught him a lesson for his slander against us", grumbled Rafiq with anger.

It is difficult to shrug the past, as history does not die. As soon as they left the station, they saw the same rickshaw puller standing before them. They tried to avoid him out of shame when he said, "I know you have missed your train and also that you do not have any money. Come I will drop you to the outskirts of the city", and reduced their discomfiture. The kindness of the rickshaw puller surprised them.

When he had gone inside the railway station to fetch water, he found these children being scolded by the TTE; he overheard the conversation and admonition; he felt their predicament. Aditya tried to refuse, but the rickshaw prevailed. The world is not so cruel as we sometimes believe.

They did not have words to express their gratitude when he dropped them and was about to scoot away silently. Their helplessness forced them to accept his generosity. A nondescript citizen struck by poverty and difficulties had his humanity intact, whereas, the rich and affluent did not care to look to the common man in the street, as if their humanity is different and their sufferings, social and physical, were of no consequence to them. The rickshaw puller was poor in means, but had a large heart to accommodate the whole world. Such diverse is humanity. Overwhelmed by the kind gesture of the rickshaw puller,

Aditya took out the watch that he had hidden, yesterday night in his pocket, and gave it to their benefactor, who accepted it after being emotionally compelled by the lad.

It was money, for which he had been breathing smoke on dirty and polluted roads of an average Indian city; he volunteered to sacrifice it for them. Strange is human nature; they had seen both devil and god in human beings within a spell of twelve hours.

He had tears in his eyes that moved even Aditya, who could not stop his own. Aditya continued to chase him with his eyes, while he was lost on the horizon. They walked for about 5 km without uttering a single word, until they reached a point where road and railroad ran parallel once again. They were tired and hungry when Aditya suggested that they should try taking lift once again. It was a welcome idea and all agreed. Soon they saw a truck coming and waved. The driver happily obliged and stopped.

"Where are you going?" asked Sayid.

"I am going to Bhopal", the driver replied.

They asked the driver to drop them at the bypass, three kilometers ahead of Dewas, as the truck was to take another route later. As soon as they got up and settled, he roared towards Dewas. He stopped at the bypass that separated their ways and asked, "What about money?" while they tried to get down, he continued hastily, "I will take thirty rupees only."

"Sorry we have no money, if we had, we would have taken train or a bus", replied Sayid.

"You penniless buggers get down", screamed the driver inflicting another blow to their self-respect. You bastards", the driver said and accelerated past them rashly.

They walked to reach the very place from where they had started their journey. The journey appeared so long, though it was so short. They were seized with great anxiety for they will have to explain – where had they been after disappearing from home.

"What would our parents and family members think of our absence?" said Aditya and continued, "I would never tell my parents that I had run away from home."

"Worrying, where have we disappeared, frantically and anxiously, they must have looked at all possible places to find us. What a mental torture we exposed them to", thought Aditya and looked pale and more worried than others. "What would my father do with me? He would probably kill me. What explanation will I give for my absence from the home last night? My father would ask, my mother, brothers, uncle and aunty and all others in my family would ask, "Where had you disappeared?" he thought. These worries kept him so occupied that he did not realize that they had reached the railway station.

Rafiq said, "Let us take different routes before somebody knew that we were together last night." They parted looking at each other crestfallen and with remorse. Lessons in life do not come without a price tag of hardships.

□

9

Aditya had scarcely walked fifty yards when he saw people were staring at him. He was walking with heavyheartedness and agony; his hands and legs were trembling nervously; he was sweating with fear and anxiety; he was not able to retain his composure and his decision-making abilities suffered. Though, his luck brought him back, but not without a taint of adventure.

One of his friends accosted him and asked, "Where were you Aditya? Your parents and your relatives have been looking for you the whole night. They have not slept and were contemplating to go to the police station to register your disappearance."

His friend tried to explain what had happened the previous night in his locality and his home. However, what explanation he would give to his parents was uppermost in his mind, which kept him so engrossed that, he could hardly pay attention to what his friend said. When his friend asked again, "Aditya, where were you the last night?" he had no answer, so frightened and bewildered he was. His home was still a few yards away, and he just did not know how to explain his absence throughout the night. He had manipulated his marks sheet not long ago to deceive his parents, what could he do this time was a big question.

Now somebody else asked, "Where were you, Aditya? Your family members were searching for you. They have not slept the whole night. Your mother is crying for you", burdening him with a fear of the unknown.

Before he could respond he discovered that he was standing in front of his home. His brother stood there; he tried to brief him what transpired in his absence and questioned, "Where were you? We were looking for you. We asked many of your friends and came to know that two others were also missing. Please come inside and for god's sake tell us where were you?" This revelation further dampened his already sagging spirits.

* * *

The night when Aditya disappeared was nothing less than a disaster for his family, particularly his parents. At around eight in the night, his father asked Aditya's younger brother, casually, "Where is Aditya?"

"I do not know", was his reply.

"Go and enquire in the area and ask his friends about him. Today, I will teach him a lesson. He is taking too much liberty these days. Enough is enough", fumed his father ruefully.

He asked everybody else in the family to enquire about him as he was away for more than two hours. He hardly left home after seven in the evening except during the festivals. His brothers and uncles were at the job to find him. His mother was worried, for she had noticed very unusual behavior and activities of her son for some days past, yet did not suspect anything serious.

When the clock struck ten and it was clear that Aditya was not to be found anywhere, they made frantic calls to all their close relatives and friends. Nobody had any clue. By midnight his father and uncles worriedly pondered over the possibility of his getting kidnapped. They were not sure where Aditya had been, for replies from friends and relatives did not offer any leads.

"Should we inform the police now?" asked one of his uncles.

Aditya's mother was sobbing, and his father admonished her to hold patience. "I think we should wait till tomorrow morning, and hope by that time the enquiries would yield some clue", said a worried father, who was not ready to entertain desperate thoughts. This was one of the worst and darkest nights in their lives. They could not sleep the whole night; mother wept, father was worried, and brothers were puzzled and everyone was distressed. It was a real nightmare.

Sayid's parents were equally worried, but waited for some news. Rafiq's family did not care much as they knew he would come back; earlier also he had left without information or permission and had returned the next day.

While Aditya's mother was lying on the bed awake, a worried and frantic father was pacing up and down in the house and others were pretending to sleep. The day arrived still good news evaded them. Neither Aditya came back nor there was any information about him. Finally, his father decided to report the matter to the police.

They discussed what should they tell to the police. They had to prepare for the impertinent questioning, because rather than solve the problem of the citizens Police in India creates more problems for the complainant. Many organs of the state in this country are continuing with the legacy of the British Raj; Police is one of them. Before the first information report is lodged, numerous questions would be put to them, and the complainants would be required to answer them, not to speak of the humiliation at the police station. The police officer would comment, "See the parental neglect is responsible for increase in the crime rate among children", use abusive and disrespectful language, and embarrass them without writing the FIR. On such occasions, citizens run to the local politician for help. A call from him with a transfer threat would discipline the police officer and compel him to register the FIR. In government, transfer is a tool of punishment against public servants, who do not listen and submit to the dictates of the masters in power.

Aditya's father would then be compelled to give bribe, though unwillingly, and the illicit money would prompt the police to act. The police officer would finally show some courtesy by accepting it and giving a copy of FIR to him. He would also order them to inform him if his son comes back, which would be sufficient indication for a beleaguered father to expect nothing more from them.

Losing a son is a trauma, but visiting a police station in this country is a greater shock. Aditya's father held the conviction that places like government offices, hospitals, police stations or the local courts are foul places.

He said once, "god spare us from humiliation and insults at these public institutions." However, now it was his turn to receive the share of disdain, disrespect, and shame of a lifetime that comes from the anger at being helpless and forlorn in such circumstances. It is so common in this country to live with dishonour and humiliation.

His parents and others, who kept vigil the whole night, did not know what had happened to Aditya. "Was he kidnapped? Did he meet with an accident? Is he still alive?" All such kinds of disturbing and morbid thoughts assailed them. In the midst of all sadness and uncertainty, they received the good news that Aditya was found, when they were heading for the police station.

His brother announced, excitedly, "Aditya has come back." The news was greeted with tears of joy. When it comes to their children, parents are the weakest beings. It was a matter of joy for the lost father, who was vastly disconcerted.

He saw his father and others waiting. A tearful but angry father asked, "Where were you the last night, my child?"

Before Aditya could say anything with his sorrowful voice, an irate father soundly thrashed him; no one intervened. Seeing his father's fury, every other family member left the room except his mother, who had only tears in her eyes, not for the beating he received, but for his safe return. She had prayed non-stop for the safe return of her son and was happy now that he finally returned.

The beating was very severe and he had bumps and bruises all over. His father beat him not for running away from home, but for the fact that he cherished great dreams of a bright future for his son. He wanted his son to achieve everything that he could not, because for him the conditions were not conducive. His son had let him down.

His hands stopped when an equivalent pain of beating one's own child, so vehemently, doused the burst of anger and shame. When Aditya had taken the last beating from his father, there was a sound of sobbing. His father's anger ended with guilt, whereas, Aditya's guilt turned into anger – anger with his own self.

With his remaining anger, Aditya's father pronounced, "He should leave his house and as a punishment go to his maternal uncle's house and make his own living."

Aditya thought of advancing several stories, but desisted, for no one would trust him, though nobody asked him, where was he the last night.

* * *

Lost and disillusioned after severe beating and bashing, Aditya fell into his mother's lap. Mothers are always full of natural and selfless love, which they wear on their sleeves; her mother was a magnanimous lady, and without enquiring what had happened to him and where he was the last night she consoled him and assured further insurance against his father's heart. She gave him the shadow of love amid the scorching heat of his father's fury.

He knew not for how long did he remain in his mother's lap when she uttered the 'golden words'.

"Do not ever give up", encouraged his mother, "you may go wherever your father sends you, but never forget that you can achieve whatever you want and become what you aspire to be, if you work hard and persevere. Never ever give up my son, never." There were tears in his eyes at the generosity of his mother.

"There are always good and rightful ways to achieve things one wants in life; a dream can become a reality with right intentions, actions and hard work. An ordinary person can also achieve extraordinary feat if he has strong determination and tenacity", she continued.

"Nothing is impossible in this world of possibilities, but first you should know for sure what you expect of your life; your aims should be clearly defined. They should not be the imposed ones. You were led away by your unmeaning adventures", continued his mother. He knew what his mother was aiming at. It was for the first time that his mother had spoken to him with maternal concerns. Perhaps, the household chores engaged her so much that she couldn't get time to speak earlier to her beleaguered child on some vital issues connected with life.

She emphasized: "First be sure what do you want of your life through meditation, introspection and reflections. Try to understand the purpose of your being on earth before determining your aim. Once you know that you can concentrate your power in that direction where destiny and divine powers drive you to achieve your goals in life."

Aditya listened to her attentively, "Now obey your father's decision, go to your maternal uncle's village, but never forget that hard work is the be all and end of life." Life is a treasure – one needs to find it; those who find it become successful; likewise those who understand the message of life reach greater heights for sure, and those who can't, fall. Life some times cannot be dictated; destiny drives it blindly, and makes human beings suffer alternating with some happiness and vengeance.

His mother left him to reflect upon her words. Her words imparted strength to his soul, that he would never resort to anything wrong or mean to achieve his goals and dreams in life. He resolved to become a lawyer and was ready to sacrifice everything to find a purpose in life.

□

Part – 2
A NEW BEGINNING

10

His cousin brothers, uncles and aunts came to meet him and his parents were concerned about him. One of them asked, "Aditya, where were you the whole night? It must have been a terrible night." When this question was repeated as a chorus it was grossly irritating. One of his cousin brothers ridiculed and mocked at him, and suggested a taint, "It must have been an adventurous experience for you, to be away for a night. Had you told me in advance, I would have accompanied you."

"Shut up", retorted his uncle, lessening the distress and Aditya felt that the volley of questions was not just their concern, but also much more than that.

"I went to see a movie with two other friends and while travelling in the train we were caught by a TTE, who took us to Indore. We were set free two hours later, once we had paid twenty-five rupees to that rapacious beast. Then we took lift in a truck to come back. We travelled in a truck for some distance then walked on foot to cover the remaining distance in the morning once we were dropped in the midway", revealed Aditya.

"Were you not afraid?" questioned a relative hearing the harrowing tale.

"I was, when we were crossing the Jungle on foot." He burst into tears that saved him from further enquiry. Tears are expressions that speak more than words. Tears provided shelter to him from the intriguing questions, which made him uncomfortable.

An unusual thing happened that night, for his father came to him, before he was going to sleep, and said, "You are allowed to stay in home, if you promise to pass the X standard with good grades, if not, you will have to leave." It was unbelievable and he nodded immediately with innocence and ignorance of a vanishing childhood. It was a respite and he promised himself to do well.

On his first day in the class, his former friends, who knew about his conspicuous absence from home for a night, came and asked about his disappearance. He felt embarrassed and preferred to be silent. After repeated failed attempts, his friends realized that it was futile to ask, for he would not reveal anything; they stopped asking him.

He studied sedulously with all his strengths, for he knew that he was not an extraordinary child, but he was also aware that he had extraordinary capacity to work hard. Pre board exams were held in December in which his performance was better than before, which his teachers also acknowledged, with pleasant surprise and disbelief. Though, he was not satisfied; he put in more efforts, solved all the previous year papers, checked them himself and observed with satisfaction that his performance had vastly improved. The final exam was one month away and he studied the whole syllabus thoroughly. He did very well.

The eagerly awaited day for the results arrived. He was flushed with pleasure when the principal congratulated and told him, for he had not only secured first division, but also secured third rank in the class of more than a hundred students. Everyone was surprised – his friends, classmates, teachers and his family members, who never expected such a brilliant performance, as he left many good students behind. Some of his teachers, who were not favourably inclined, were astonished at his grades. He became a role model for them, to be quoted time and again, to encourage the weak students. A teacher, who had scolded him, and had thrown him out of the class once, was the one to enjoy the occasion most.

His friends, who had doubted his abilities, were surprised and awed at his singular performance. Both his parents were the happiest and delighted on his achievement. Their worries gave way to pride and a belief that he would carve out his place in life.

The score of seventy-four percent was a phenomenal jump of twenty percent over his previous year performance. His achievement should not be viewed from the absolute, but should be judged by the quantum of jump in ranks and numbers he had achieved. The matter was not yet over as he still had a lot to prove, for he evinced that an average child is equally capable of achieving merit at par with bright students. Now no one could take him lightly.

After the results new relations emerged. Most of them had chosen the direction of their higher studies. The unfortunate ones, who flunked, left the school. Aditya chose to remain in the same school and did not shift to the so-called elite school. Those who failed, like his friends Rafiq and Sayid, left the school. He made new friends – Basant, Danny, and Raju, who had one thing in common – love of food and their friendship grew.

He passed eleventh standard with good marks.

* * *

It was the start of a new session and it was going to be his last year in the school, before setting out to the unchartered territories, hunting a dream career of his choice. Then one day he had new friends Brajesh and his sister. Their father was a government servant and was transferred from Patna. She was the same girl whom he had once seen in Patna, but did not have the courage to talk. Since she was his classmate now, he introduced himself, "hi, I am Aditya."

"Hello, I am Arpita. If I am not mistaken you had come to play in Patna", she replied, as if it was a happening of yesterday. He blushed and said, "You are right. I am the same person. Nice to meet you again." He could not believe that the girl, with whom he was momentarily attracted and could not talk due to adolescent shyness, had come back in his life.

She was to become part of his close friend circle. He fostered great love for her, but couldn't summon up courage to tell her. It is not that age when youngsters foster passionate love and all that they can boast of is a romantic attachment, called infatuation.

Akash was an intelligent student, who always remained ahead of Aditya in the class and examinations. He was an extrovert, who would express his thoughts so effortlessly that others were jealous of him. Aditya had a seat next to him. Arpita frequented them after every period.

"How are your studies going on for the monthly exams?" asked Arpita.

"Fairly good", they replied.

"Will you take part in the debate competition next week?"

"Yes", they replied simultaneously looking at each other.

They became good friends. Adtiya expected so much from her not knowing why.

* * *

One day he went back to the classroom to pick up his forgotten football kit, and what he saw was incredibly shocking and depressing. He saw Arpita curled in Akash's arms with their lips locked passionately. He was caressing her hair and was searching for her breasts. While they remained clung to each other, his hands discovered her beautiful anatomy, while she was fondling his manly breast beneath the open shirt. Stunned, he left the place in disbelief without picking up anything. He abhorred the moment. He went straight to the canteen not to eat, but for seclusion, though, eating relieves pain and sorrow. He sat desolately, frozen in a sad mood, while his friends searched for him. He wept in loneliness.

He had only one companion close to him – Raju – to share and mourn with. He told him everything he saw. "That explains her absence from the sports field. When the whole class was playing or enjoying on the field, they were enjoying each others company", Raju said ruefully and continued, "This blighter Akash has hijacked someone else's love."

"I myself should be blamed for this and not him. I was too busy to attend to my love."

"Life goes on, and never waits for any one, big or small, man or child", said Raju consoling and pitying him at the same time.

Aditya became restless; he could not control his emotions now. After lunch he went straight to her and asked a stupid adolescent driven question, "Do you love Akash?"

"What are you talking about?" she was surprised.

"Please tell me if it is true or not that you love him?" he repeated.

"Yes, but why are you asking this? What has it to do with you?" she replied, petulantly.

He left her and the classroom suddenly, clearly showing his disappointment on learning that she fell in love with Akash, who was nobody's buddy in the entire class, for he was an uppity. She adored him. He recalled the moment when their eyes had met during the tournament in Patna. He now regretted why did he go to Patna in the first place. How excited was he on her arrival in the school. She was his first love that withered before it blossomed. He was sad and dejected. That day while going back home, he sat quiet in the bus, shedding tears. It was raining, and none noticed his moist eyes.

He felt a grim loneliness. The darkness was lonely and the loneliness was so dark and deep that no light could venture into the deep most recesses of his lost soul. He thought, "A soul could not evoke emotions in a rigid heart that is emotionless, heartless, and is the very embodiment of a desert where no flowers blossom." With the betrayal of a solemn promise of a lasting love by a mortal soul, it was not only a heart that was broken, but also a faith that was shattered, the faith in the idol of that lonely temple called love. One more individual had fallen and again a promise was broken. So sad and alone his bruised heart was, so much hurt, that the feelings of loss overpowered his senses to the extent of numbness of the soul.

At some moments the heart weeps, emotions get affected and the lover remains a picture of sorrow – sorrow that bitterly hurts him, as it reaches the innermost depths of his heart, even his soul.

That night he wept for letting out his feelings known to his beloved. It is more than fast friendship between man and woman; after all even God meant it – when he created human beings.

□

11

It was the Annual Day celebration in the school. Aditya, Basant, Danny, Raju and Arpita were discussing their future plans sitting among empty desks.

"I am thinking of pursuing engineering", said Danny. Arpita wanted to seek technical education.

"I will go to Kota, to prepare for getting admission in an IIT", said Basant.

"I am planning to go with Basant", said Danny.

"I know my caliber, so I will join some engineering college in our state itself", said Raju.

"I will go to New Delhi for my higher studies", said Aditya and he stunned everybody, "I will opt for Political Science for further studies."

"Why are you planning for Political Science?" asked Arpita.

"I want something different in my life. I want not to run after an engineer's job. I have decided to seek a career in law. I have got only one life so I want to do what I love the most; nay what my father, or my brother wants me to do."

His choice surprised them. There was complete silence for a moment, for they all looked at him in disbelief. Such an ambition surprised them, as they all were privileged offspring of officers under whom his father had worked. They suffered from a sense of misplaced superiority, which was under threat.

"I want to join politics later", revealed Aditya, which came as another shocker for his friends.

"All the best in you venture", replied Danny, sarcastically.

Though they were astonished, and could hardly believe that he would achieve what he was speaking about, they thought it to be a mere wishful thinking of middle class Aditya. However, Arpita reacted differently. She was more egalitarian than others in the list of his friends. Abilities, competence and hard work are not the monopoly of the great and well to do. It is surprising that adolescents could also think like a hardened human being, who has acquired all the ills, that plague a divided society – a society divided by religion, caste and colour.

Prejudices do not develop overnight, but is a systematic inculcation of habit through the process of learning and socialization when a child grows into an adult. Prejudices once developed take generations to die. Till they die, generations suffer injustices at the hands of the oppressors, who use prejudices as the justification for the injustices inflicted on them, and tyranny and tirades to suppress them. They were friends, but they had their basic instincts that create both a good and a bad citizen. Sometimes they generate competition, prejudices, selfishness, indifference, hatred and contempt, but at other times create friendship, care, altruism, concern, love and sacrifice.

In the board exams of X standard, Aditya had overtaken most of the newly made friends. They were trying to forget their discomfiture under the guise of friendship. Year and a half had passed after the results and they had now become chummy friends. However, this revelation had reinvigorated the unthinkable, unimaginable and unbearable injury this lad had inflicted on them.

"What do you want, if studying engineering fails to achieve your goals in life? There are better job opportunities for technically qualified professionals. I will complete engineering course here and then, perhaps, go to the USA for further studies", said Basant, who on many instances had expressed his desire, relying on the support of his uncle, who worked in the Silicon Valley.

Raju interrupted their discussion and reminded them that the function was to start. The annual function was a culmination of the cumulative efforts of all the students interested in extra-curricular activities. They had rehearsed so many times before presenting it to the gathering of students and their parents, teachers and other dignitaries.

Late night the function ended with the message of friendship and respect for teachers. The feelings were mixed as they were boarding the buses to leave for their homes; some were going with their parents, who came to see their performances in their private vehicles. They also had a feeling of anxiety, as the final exams were fast approaching.

* * *

Aditya studied with renewed enthusiasm and excelled once again. This time he stood first in the class, further increasing the agony and dismay of his competitors, who now had started looking at him with envy and respect. He scored ninety-one percent marks, quite an unexpected performance. Accidently, one may excel once or twice, but if the performance is constant then one is compelled to acknowledge the merit of the student. He enjoyed overtaking Akash hedonistically, as if it was a sort of revenge.

His graph of excellence in studies continued to rise even further. His mother's profound words were to fill his life, as they were the words of wisdom and of love that would be a beacon and a lighthouse to guide him in the rest of his life. The pain, anger, guilt and disrespect he suffered from the cruel people on that terrific night of misadventure and shame had taught him a precious lesson.

His success though, not phenomenal, gave big boost to his spirits. It encouraged him and boosted his morale in winning many hearts. Those who hated him for being delinquent in the past now treated him with respect and awe. He became a favorite of those who berated him for being delinquent; he encouraged others also, especially weak and laggard students, who started believing that anything is possible. His teachers started expressing that, "one may participate in sports, extracurricular activities, enjoy life, commit mistakes and at the same time perform well in studies." The shortsighted teachers believed that studies and excellence were the preserve of a selected few and hailed the view that studies should be given paramount importance.

He decided to study in the prestigious Delhi University, which by far was the best place for higher studies. He was tossing between selection and rejection after his name did not appear in the first cut-offs, but luckily a seat fell vacant, and he was admitted in the second cut-off. He was lucky to be admitted to the 'Hindu College' of Delhi University – one of the best by all counts. It was a moment to rejoice for his parents, as good future and opportunities waited him. They hardly knew that he had different plans.

□

12

After getting admission and spending few days at home Aditya prepared to leave for Delhi to continue his higher studies. When the day arrived for him to leave his home for the first time, his mother had tears in her eyes. She said, "Look after yourself." His brother said teasingly, "I am happy that it will not be required to share things with someone from now on" and hugged him with moist eyes. He replied, "you have to be a topper in the class this time also." His father did not say much except, "study well, and whenever you need extra money, please inform me before the tenth of every month".

His father dropped him at the Bus Station; he did not look back; his eyes had welled up with tears. He reached Bhopal from where he had to board the train for Delhi.

It was a bright and sunny afternoon, when the sun was at its best, heating the earth and the air, and charring the people, who were getting exposed to that scorching heat. The station was packed with thousands of aspirants, who after visiting Bhopal, to appear in the recruitment exams for employment in railways, and blistered by unbearable heat, were returning back to their respective places as far as Rajasthan, Uttar Pradesh, Bihar, and Maharashtra and from wherever they came. They wore a tired smile on their faces with 'May Heat' and were confused about which train they should catch. They were giving a run to police personnel deployed to maintain order at the station.

Some of these aspirants were sleeping on the dirty floor of the railway station, full of filth and shit, some were eating, some were chatting, some were discussing and some others were quarrelling over trifles. The discussions were about difficulty levels and contents of the examination paper, high temperatures, and two foreigners waiting for the Shatabdi Express.

In India whenever and wherever people see foreigners they presume that they are from Britain. The British rule has left, surely, a deep impact on Indian psyche that people are still obsessed with white skin and English language. People surround them as if they were awful aliens.

Somebody commented on these foreigners, "they are so lucky that their land permits them early sex, whereas in India people live a puritan life without bodily pleasures, till our youth vanishes, and our parents get us tied to grooms and bridegrooms of their choice", at which others giggled.

"Indians think that all the foreigners are rich and ladies are easily available and ever ready for free-sex as shown in English movies", mumbled another annoyed educated person, waiting for the TTE to provide him an accommodation in the packed appearing train with his unconfirmed ticket. Another one who didn't like his fellow countrymen looking at foreigners with such perverted thoughts said, "if they were rich they would go to Australia, New Zealand, USA or a European country, why come to a poor country like India." India may be a poor country wealth wise but culturally not many advanced can match it.

A young lady in her teens walked in towards the platform, hastily, to catch the train and made her way through the crowds of people at the station. Amidst her worried moves, she caught the attention of this young lad, Aditya, still in his teens, was trying to avoid baton-wielding police constables that were guarding the station and hit everybody presuming them to be aspirants.

The train arrived; passengers de-boarded, while porters assisted them to unload their heavy luggage. The police had difficult time to allow the passengers to come out of the compartment, for those who wanted to board the train, were jostling at the door. The police provided room to the rich and influential passengers.

Aditya, made his way to the TTE to get a seat. "Sir, I am on the waiting list."

"There is no berth or seat available."

"Sir, it is important for me to reach Delhi."

"How am I concerned."

"Sir, please help."

"Pay five hundred", he said in a quite voice, glancing around to ensure nobody else heard.

"What?" reacted Aditya, skeptically.

"Five hundred if you want to strike a deal. There are many passengers in the queue." He had no choice but to pay; he acquired a seat. It is sometimes easy to arrange a seat by paying a little bribe to the railway ticket collector than lawfully getting a confirmed ticket. Corruption begins when the needy and the helpless surrenders to the corrupt even though reluctantly; this is how corruption begins. Aditya was wondering that there was no space on the platform, but the train had lot of room to accommodate the one who could bribe.

He relaxed on his seat. His thoughts went back to that beautiful girl wearing a worried smile. If it were not such a pathetic day he could have seen the girl at his heart full.

While surveying the compartment he found the same lady, who had caught his attention on the platform, and to his surprise she was coming towards him now. She settled on the seat next to him for that was her allotted seat. She was a comely lady with a beautiful shinning face, and an even forehead on which her curly hair played. She had beautiful eyes and even the glasses she wore could not hide the glamour of her eyes and cheeks. She had thin lips and seductive creamy cheeks. She wore blue jeans and a white sleeveless shirt.

When their eyes met, they looked at each other and were lost for a brief spell. There was romance in the air. Such coincidences sometimes bloom into rare companionship.

She seemed to be a reserved person, but the loneliness of the compartment threw good companionship. The talk started with the I-Pod, playing music in her ears. It was an eight Gigabyte I-Pod with video features. An item alien to him, though he had heard of it, but could not afford. She showed him its features and some photographs stored in it.

"All these were taken during a party with school mates", she said.

He identified a person in the photograph and commented, "So that's your buddy."

"No. He is a gay", she replied.

It was an obvious relief. She was holding the book titled "Da Vinchi Code" authored by Dan Brown. The Vatican and its followers had proscribed Dan Brown's novel for being very imaginative to hurt feelings and emotions of people.

"Do you find it interesting?"

"Don't know."

"It is an interesting novel, only after you venture beyond seventy pages", he said. She was reading the fiftieth page.

"Did you read Jane Austen?" She asked.

"No."

"What other writers have you read?"

"I have read Charles Dickens, Naipaul, Arundhati Roy, Amartya Sen, and Salman Rushdie and many more."

"You read only famous and popular ones, is it to impress me?"

"I believe, in the limited time I get I should read those novels and books which have been favourably reviewed. Why should I impress you?" he said, innocently.

"One may read literature of one's choice, but sometimes it is good to read the lesser writers too. They hold surprises."

"Where is the time for extra reading? I have never claimed to be a voracious reader."

"Have you read Amitav Ghosh?"

"No", he replied.

She told him about a recent novel of Amitav Ghosh and then they discussed other novels also dwelling upon religion, vegetarianism and travelling. Now the lady was gradually feeling comfortable with him.

There was something more in their meeting. Some coincidences set the stage for further discussion, as per current state of her residence both of them belonged to the same place and both were of the same age.

Aditya inferred from the air-ticket, she was keeping as a bookmark, that her name was Puja Ghosh. She unbundled her hair and spread them over her neck beautifully. She could not believe the integrity and naive charm he had. This brought her even closer and share not so trivial issues like people fast loosing their virginity in teens, innumerable rapes happening in the country and the rights of homosexuals. She was feeling the warmth of his company, though she was not sure of her feelings; she had met so many people, but with him there was something special. Their conversation centered round studies and job opportunities and no personal issues were mentioned that made both of them comfortable.

Aditya thought, "Should I tell the pretty lady that I am going to take admission in a college in Delhi and job is not of any reckoning for me."

Something stopped him. May be he was talking to a very open and modern lady, who would not mind talking to a man with average background. He had never felt such closeness and satisfaction while talking to a lady of genius in his past interactions with anyone. He was increasingly becoming restless amid the warm exchange of ideas, events, and discussions and particularly about the familiarity arising in a rare coincidental encounter. Nobody ever sat besides her with so much ease; he too was never so much comfortable, when a lady sat by his side; he felt extremely pleasant, though nervous.

"Once I was followed during night time when I was riding my scooty. Though, the followers chasing me did not know that my parents were escorting me in their car at some distance", she said and continued, "the followers teased me and when I told my father about the chase, he stopped the person in his thirties and berated him. Incidentally, he was my father's subordinate and begged to be forgiven. My father yelled in response, 'You are a married man and do such things, shame on you'. They turned tail and ran away.

"Something is seriously wrong with the society that ill-treats its females. The male bias in our society is demolishing womanhood resulting in the decline of sex ratio. The day is not far when we would be hunting females in foreign lands", he said that made them laugh.

"She is intelligent, beautiful and for all purposes a comely person and why should she get interested in an unemployed youth", he wondered.

He was tossed back to life when she questioned, "Where do you stay and what your parents do?"

"I am from Dewas", he said, "my father is an accountant. What about you?" he dared.

"My father is a Brigadier in the Indian Army."

She could sense a discomfort and nervousness in his voice.

"That is wonderful", he blurted out after getting his composure back.

The train stopped at many places, but they hardly noticed. As the train approached the final destination, their discussion centered round country, communalism, backwardness of different communities, but beneath that formality there was something unusual. It seemed, as if they had known each other for ages.

The Shatabdi Express was nearing Delhi fast. Though, by international standards no train qualifies to be superfast, until it could run at an average speed of two hundred kilometers per hour, ironically Indian Railways get satisfaction by calling it superfast. They were still talking while gazing out of the windshield to escape each other's sight.

Finally, the train reached Delhi. She offered to drop him home, but he declined gracefully. He helped her to get down and reach the car. They said bye-bye to each other and left as strangers. They parted without exchanging address or mobile number, which is usual at such meetings.

He pondered over the encounter with that stranger, and wondered what could have been his fate if he were still in school and sharing this close shave with his naughty friends. □

13

He took a taxi and as it moved away from the railway station, he saw through the dirty windshield of that old taxi, which appeared new from outside, wide roads, beautiful buildings, sign boards and lights. He had come to Delhi twice, but had never seen the city so closely.

He reached the hostel to find a single room accommodation. One could compare it with the cell in a jail, where convicts spend a long term for some unknown crime.

People from rich families hardly stayed in these hostels. Most of the students from good families stayed outside the campus in better accommodations including flats and rooms as paying guests. Aditya did not want to press his parents to the extremes; consequently he stayed in hostel – a price he had to pay for having the courage to pursue his dreams to excel in the chosen field of his endeavour.

On entering the room he saw a pair of clothes hanging on the wall, a mosquito net fixed over a cot lying in one corner of the room. He barely settled to relax when somebody knocked at the door. He opened the door to find a six feet tall and handsome lad standing in front of the door. Aditya was surprised to see him. Before entering the room, he failed to notice the place adjacent to the door, where two names were written on an old plate. He thought that this room was meant for him alone.

"I am your roommate", said the six feet tall young man.

He gave way to him to enter in the room and said "Sorry I did not know that you were my roommate."

"There is no need for apologies. I am Parag Shekhar."

"I am Aditya."

"I belong to Bihar, though my family is staying in Bhopal, since my father works in BHEL as Superintendent Engineer."

"What a coincidence, I am also from Madhya Pradesh. My father is an Accountant in Bank Note Press in Dewas."

They discussed about their school days and what made them come to Delhi for higher studies. They talked for about half an hour and liked each other. Parag, he hoped, would prove to be one of the best friends in the college after his adolescent friendship ended in a disaster during school days.

They got up in the morning and prepared for the class. It was his first day in the college and his seniors ragged him. He was told that ragging would continue for a month; he was disappointed.

* * *

A little before Nine O'clock most of the students were already settled in the classroom, anticipating an interesting lectures. It was time for the class to begin. They were discussing with each other about various places they came from, the books they had to buy, their plans to enjoy life in the college. A bald-headed, sedate old man entered the class; he was the professor of Comparative Politics. The professor was decently dressed. His black trouser was in perfect contrast to the shirt. He had scanty moustache and a big jaw; he was bespectacled. His entry calmed the babbling.

The class started with usual gaiety in the classroom that was big enough to accommodate all the students. The walls were painted light yellow with the lower half studded with woodwork. The seating arrangement was in the shape of an open rectangle made with tables followed by inflexible chairs –inflexible enough to ensure that students do not fall asleep, but they still slept. Some books were placed on the tables to show the earnestness of the students towards "happy learning" process.

The Professor stood on an elevated platform to see that the students were listening, and not sleeping; though it didn't matter to the students, as they had the habit of sleeping with open eyes. This is one thing they learned to counter the kind of learning that India promoted. The lecture was on "Political evolution of the Superpowers". He began without any annotations or introductions:

"A simple analysis of the facts tells that the countries which we call great today stand on a solid foundation. The units of the social, political and economic systems stand on this pillar with other sub-units standing in total synchronism. As China is emerging as a counterweight to the USA, its economy seems to be totally integrated with every unit providing support to the other."

"Sir, China has a different political system compared to the USA even then it is developing. Is there some link between development and the kind of political system?" someone asked impairing the smoothness of his deliberations.

"We will come to that point once we take up political systems of different countries", replied a visibly agitated professor, who was more concerned about his lecture than answering. Giggles followed at his reply and the class was dead silent once again, as if paying homage to someone.

"Our understanding becomes more clear when we observe that these world powers have strong agricultural economy, though, it may not be a significant proportion of the overall GDP. It makes them almost independent in the food grain production. Though, their cost of production varies significantly which compels them to spend huge amount in subsidies on agriculture. On this foundation stands a solid pillar of state political system, which provides continuity." He continued.

He pointed to Parag and asked, "you in the corner! Don't sleep! Tell me how does economy and defense contribute in making a country become superpower?"

"Sir I feel economy provides monetary capability to invest in defense that makes a country strong", responded Parag. However, Professor did not say anything leaving him and the class dumbstruck.

"Different segments of industries stand firm on such sub-structure and make a sound economic system. Defense provides strength like steel to these pillars and thus, preserves the structure. This is one of the easiest presentations of the facts", he boasted.

"Sir can you give another example?" asked a girl sitting next to Parag, courteously.

"Another simple comparison makes the understanding of the topic apparent. Countries in the West Asia, generally, depend on other countries for food. These countries have great reserves of petroleum, enough to become rich. However, it must be noted that they are not called as superpower, even if they are among the richest in the world, since their dependence on food prevents them to take independent stand." He explained, showing his erudition, without any concern for students' presence, or their understanding of the subject in the class. Though, he felt delighted to advice his students, whenever the occasion so desired.

They hardly understood anything and looked foolish, for his lecture was confusing and it appeared as if the engine was running away, blowing siren and leaving the coaches behind.

While the class was going on Aditya's eyes collided with two other eyes through thin lenses. He could not believe the coincidence. That was Puja, the same girl whom he had met in the train while coming to Delhi. He was possessed with strange, but delightful feelings on seeing her, when the boredom and incomprehension of the lecture was gone.

After the class, Aditya and Parag interacted with Neha, Sam, Param and Sunny who were sitting on the next benches and looked equally confused. They got acquainted with each other and were friends soon; they would remain a cohesive group throughout their college days. Aditya tried to move towards Puja, to greet her with excitement that they had met before, but she seemed to be indifferent and left the class.

The classes continued so did the studies. Aditya could not believe that Puja was the same lady whom he had met in the train since he was not able to talk to her freely. She was a changed person.

* * *

Puja remained aloof, may it be elections or any other issue – her indifference was apparent. One day she was reading about French revolution in the library when Aditya joined her. He claimed, "Why read about this? I can explain you."

"What?" she was surprised to see his interruption. Nevertheless, he continued, "Justice requires sustainability and equilibrium among various forces. This requires a very simple solution, but is very difficult to implement."

"What is that solution?" she asked, entering into a discussion, almost forgetting that they were in the library.

"Justice calls for equitable distribution of the resources, not forcefully, but by genuine efforts. These efforts include building the capabilities of the destitute to enable them to sustain their life, which eventually would reduce the discrepancies and inequalities. An employee shouldn't be exploited only for want of his inability to take risk. Thus, equilibrium is possible when a weaker person is made capable of producing valuable services to the society."

"Are you talking of some utopian world?"

"Not exactly. But, it ensures a sustainable relationship between a mighty employer and an employee, the rich and the poor and various other classes for peaceful existence."

"Would then it require coercion?"

"With justice, I do not intend to advocate that the property of the rich be confiscated and distributed, forcefully. But, some percentage of profit may invariably be given to the people, who are an integral part of the production process, to the extent of producer's satisfaction."

"It is already practiced in many big companies."

"Yes, especially, the Information Technology firms, which have a program of Employee Stock Ownership Plan. It has made such companies grow faster than their competitors. It is also evident that people slog for a company, till they believe that they are receiving what they deserved or else they quit."

"Does that mean profit sharing?"

"Yes, why not. A rich businessman exploiting the labour for production and giving him or her peanuts is no justice. It leads to conflicts. They may be white collar or blue collar or any collar. World would not come to peace, and sustainability would not be achieved, until this justice is given to the needy."

"You speak like a socialist. But, how does that fit in here?"

He responded, "The world order itself has become exploitative by not giving the due to the people", She quietly watched him, who was at his best as if speaking before an audience in a debating competition, and he continued, "The existing system of unequal distribution can be traced to this uneven ownership established by the protagonists of the private property. Such exploitation is the being practiced by one and all, countries, private and even public enterprises, institutions and so on. The system of the market and the society is flawed for extending such exploitative system. The so-called entrepreneurs are amassing great wealth by taking the services of their employees."

"Then, the natural question is whether the employees deserve only the salaries or the collective ownership? Another question is, does the wealth created by entrepreneurs belong to them? The reasons may be the lifetime effort they put to establish the empire, the extra amount of risk, which might be the risk of life and pain they undergo, their extraordinary talent, which almighty has gifted them, and any other reason sufficient to defend the exploitation", she said.

They were madly lost in the discourse and as he spoke further, someone reminded them, "Please see the notice above". He looked at the board that read, "Please do not disturb others in the library", while "Please maintain silence" was written on the other one.

She said, "Why disturb people here? I will meet you in the cafeteria in fifteen minutes."

After half an hour, while he was waiting, she came and sat on the other side of the table. He ordered coffee and said, "Since the day you joined the college, I have not seen you interact with anyone, though I know you to be very talkative, specially when we met for the first time."

"I want to concentrate on my studies, I have only one goal before me."

"That explains your conspicuous absence from every activity. But, you may still make friends."

"Who told you that I do not have friends? I have – I have Neha, who is my best friend. Shall I make friends with your permission?"

Ignoring her sarcasm he ventured to ask, "What is that goal?"

"I want to be an Indian Administrative Service officer."

"An IAS, good."

"Yes."

"I appreciate that, but I still feel you can make friends."

"What do you want to say?"

"I want to say that we can be friends." He came directly to the point.

Though smitten, she preferred to be aloof and said, "I am afraid you may find me to be a depressing companion."

"It does not matter to me when I know you to be the one I met in the train."

She laughed and said, "I will consider that." They finished coffee, sat without saying anything for some time and left for the class.

It was difficult to imagine that they had met before joining the college. They kept on coming to cafeteria at this time and enjoyed coffee together almost every day and became good friends. Both liked each other, since they met, but never admitted it. His initiative to express himself to build a new relationship was lost in the crosscurrents of fear and hope of the future. Aditya now ensured that he gave at least one hour everyday to the studies in the library, where he read about world history and various revolutions.

Soon the exams for the first year were announced. They all passed. Puja topped the class. Parag came second. Aditya was tenth and Param barely passed, while others performed better than Param.

□

14

Aditya and Param participated in many debating competitions and won most of them. The elections to the student council of the college were scheduled in the month of August. They decided to contest and got involved in the elections for the college parliament.

"I have decided to contest for the post of Prime Minister, said Aditya.

"What will then become of me?" asked Param.

"You should fight for the Member of Central Council and then we can fight under one banner." Param agreed and they decided to contest for the post of the Prime Minister and the Member respectively. Being close friends they struck this arrangement.

A rich man's son Victor was contesting against Aditya for the post of the Prime Minister, while his pal Mahesh Pandey was contesting for the post of the Member. Victor was arrogant and shrewd.

* * *

One day these friends sat in the canteen to finalize their candidature when Parag warned them, "They could go to any extent to win."

"Let them try. We are not going to yield so easily. Besides, I will not use any mean tactics", exclaimed Aditya.

"I am not telling you to become corrupt to win, but we should expose their tricks and foul means and be careful of them", responded Parag.

"I agree with him", said Param while others also acquiesced. Their team included Sam, Parag, Neha and Sunny. Sam and Parag's job would be to see if their opponents were indulging in mean tactics like bribing the voters, threatening them or luring them. Sunny was to take care of their advertisement campaign, and Neha was to design the strategy for one to one contact program, prepare debate and speech in consultation with Aditya.

"Have you decided the topic for debate, which is scheduled before election? " asked Neha.

"I will opt to speak on industrial peace."

"It will be too conservative", opined Parag.

"I feel students may like it in the backdrop of the labour unrests in the recent past. "

"What? Do you want to establish communism?" interjected Parag.

"I never meant that. I am not pressing for the establishment of communism or socialism, nor am I against capitalism; I want to emphasize on industrial justice. I am not saying that everything an owner has produced be divided among the people nor am I saying that the owner be deprived of their right to own. However, a more equitable system can reduce the artificial class divisions existing since time immemorial. "

"This class-divide figures prominently in Marx's work. The solution to these class divisions have not been found so far, leading to frequent loss of industrial peace with repercussions on the societal peace, psychological and physical well being of the society", informed Neha.

"Yes, the ultimate freedom and emancipation would come, when this injustice stops and sustainability is achieved which will not come with one system alone, but when all the forces balance each other", said Aditya and argued, "Everything is a product of time. Marx is nothing, but a product of time. There is great link between the past and the present. A place producing a particular kind of philosophy, ideology, or social structure is determined by the past, for the future remains tied to the past through present, thus can't be ignored. Man produces the ideology, which in turn produces faction this faction then supports the ideology, and sometimes ideologies create great divide. Ideologies create structure that sustains itself."

"How? What kind of structure you are talking about?" asked Neha while Parag gave a disinterested look.

"Development follows a pyramidal structure, though it might have a distorted form. The USA is a case in point, it continues to be an epitome of capitalism; the unique style of working of men there created an ideology and this ideology is now creating men to sustain it; thus, it is producing capitalists and supporting capitalism throughout the world, consciously or unconsciously. It has become self-sustaining. This fact is evident in Russia and China also, which are the example of communism, though the situation is fast changing there. This can be generalized to any other country, which can be identified with some or the other unique ideology", said Aditya.

"Is Marxism the reasons for so much of discord in the world?" asked Param.

"Though, it produced conflicts, Marxism provided relief to the working classes too, by highlighting their difficulties and their despair. It had, however, created a limited world for them where they could not reach the condition of equilibrium, thus conflicts ensue. It cannot be denied that Marx's thoughts on communism have made the conditions of workers better; it has given them great bargaining power to increase their clout in getting decision made in their favour", replied Aditya.

"But people claim that Marxism has failed", said Parag, who was always uncomfortable with communism.

"Whenever any thinker develops a theory that predicts an outcome for the society, it helps in correcting the course of action. This happened with the theory propounded by Marx also, though now people reject his theories, and claim that his predictions have failed to prove. However, critics neglect that due to his predictions, the proletariat or the working classes got enlightened and resorted to secure their rights; they had asserted their rights and got them enforced. Realizing the dangers of the class conflicts the capitalists and the governments took corrective measures to avoid the confrontations leading to losses. This auto-correction has led the Marxian theory to remain only partially true. However, it should not be forgotten that if corrections had not taken place then his predictions might have become a reality – a gory reality. Societies that do not change, perish", responded Aditya.

"Is that the reason for our country having no ideology?" ridiculed Parag.

"No, we do have an ideology."

"What is that?"

"Hey guys, let us stop it here and reserve it for a future debate", requested Neha, who feared a heated discussion and pointless arguments might spoil the mood, while Parag remained obdurate and asked annoyingly, "Is it some revolution? Are you some statesmen or what?"

"A New Revolution hence begins from now on and it will not stop until the goal is achieved. The justice given to the people in this manner may dilute the authority of nation state for the reason that people or rather worker would remain satisfied and the conflict arising due to the inequitable distribution of resources would reduce drastically", declared Aditya. While others laughed and cheered him, Parag accused teasingly, "You are a communist and I am a capitalist, thus I support you not anymore, henceforth, I will vote for someone else."

"Can you do that to your good friend?" questioned Param, trying to create some more ripples. "No", was Parag's response to conclude the matter.

They worked hard to approach all the voters, apprised them of their views, and distributed leaflets and other material conveying their ideas through the manifesto. They went to all the hostels and requested the resident students to vote for them.

* * *

Victor was bent upon to do something desperate.

It was an unpleasant night. Param was tired and was shivering with fever so he decided to leave earlier than others after another hectic day. He was returning back to the hostel after finishing his work. It was dark there and visibility was almost non-existent. A distant light was visible that lighted the route between the common hall and the hostel. He was hurrying when somebody appeared before him, whom he could not recognize. He stopped him, standing before him obstructing the path.

"Who are you?" asked Param and tried to see him and found a person with his face covered with a cloth to hide his identity. Guessing what would soon follow, he tried to turn his tail, but found two more persons emerge and block his way.

"We are your bad time", answered an image.

Sound of a bang! Three more shadows merged, pounded on him, assaulted him, and when he tried to scream one of them stuffed his mouth with a cloth. He was hit hard in the stomach. He was threatened with dire consequences if the group did not withdraw their nominations; learning him unconscious, they fled, triumphantly.

While returning to the hostel Parag spotted Param, he called other friends and immediately rushed him to the hospital. Param was unconscious and was drenched in blood; he suffered five stitches on head and a broken elbow.

"There is nothing serious. I have prescribed the medicines. He will be all right, however it will take a month or so for him to recover fully", said the Doctor while the anxious friends listened.

They were agitated at this ghastly attack and were seized with an impulse to destroy Pandey. They were sure when Parag said, "It must be Pandey, who has done it at Victor's instigation." Aditya consoled them and advised not to repeat the stupidity; he restrained them and explained, "If we behave like them then what is the difference between them and us, especially, in the minds of fellow students." Next day the news of attack spread like fire. Aditya asked his supporters not to make it an issue, as it was not known who had attacked Param, though there were obvious suspects.

"I have requested police to register an FIR", he informed. They did not succumb. However, they decided to remain in groups in future.

A day remained for voting when a debate was scheduled at college auditorium in the evening. This was to take place in the presence of the whole college including teachers. Victor spoke for half an hour, and was applauded. When Aditya spoke, he was given a standing ovation. It reflected the mood of the college, but eleventh hour tactics by Victor were not known. Helpless as they were, they decided not to do anything desperate.

* * *

Voting was over and the day of counting and declaration of the results arrived. The professor in charge of elections had invited them to observe the counting procedures. After an hour of exercise, the counting was over and the results were announced. Aditya was declared the Prime Minister of the Student Council of the College and Param, the Member of the central council of Delhi University. It was their first election win. Hearing the results there was applause, cheer and rejoicing.

After few days, there was a dastardly sexual assault on a woman in Delhi, and she was thrown on the street to die. Aditya and his team decided to launch protest to ensure justice for her and to press the government to increase the safety of the women. They organized candle light vigil, postcard campaign and a march to the India gate. They continuously protested for two weeks during which they were beaten and sent to the jail. It however, helped in generating public opinion to put pressure on the authorities to ensure such crimes were not repeated with impunity, and women were provided sufficient safety on roads.

In another gruesome incident, when one of his college juniors from the Northeastern state went missing, he launched a campaign to put pressure on the police department to search for him and nail the culprits. His campaign helped in finding the student, who was kidnapped by some criminals for ransom, and was beaten severely for two days in their custody; he remained in the hospital for more than a month.

Aditya's social activities proved his mettle.

□

15

It was a dark day when black clouds enveloped the whole city, the college in particular. It seemed that it might rain heavily. Parag and Aditya were enjoying coffee in the college canteen, which was full of students chattering like birds.

"Everybody is selfish in the world and people work only for themselves", said Parag thoughtfully, like an enlightened sage, after his girlfriend broke up with him.

"The human behaviour is surprisingly strange. Man feels threatened by the individualism of another man. Though, he knows it deep down his heart, but fears expressing it. This insecurity lies in the very nature of selfishness. Since man is concerned about himself first, whether or not he accepts this, he feels insecure on seeing another individualistic person. This is a self-contradiction, as man hates another man's selfishness due to his egocentricity. In fact, when people behave naturally they appear selfish. If you found her to be selfish, should you also not understand that she was honest in her relationship with you", said Aditya to comfort an agitated Parag, sensing his spoiled mood.

"How do you know I am talking about a girl?" asked Parag, who was surprised by Aditya's revelations.

"Because you look like the one, who has suffered at the hands of a girl", said Aditya playfully, "in this physical world the relationships are governed by brute, insensitive and naked power, or in other words by force, if spoken in the language of science, precisely the principles of forces as propounded by Newton in the laws of gravity and motion."

"Your ideas are not clear to me, please enlighten me, wise man", commented Parag, flirtatiously, while Neha, Param and Sam also joined them.

Aditya smiled and continued, "See Parag, your ex-girlfriend must have felt that you have none better than her and therefore is worth nothing, so she left you."

"And you are some kind of astrologer predicting that. But you are damned right."

"I am only stating the facts the way I understand them. Every one of us has something or the other to learn from everybody else. One needs to open his eyes to learn."

"What do you call your predictions?" asked Neha, jokingly.

"I call it theory of potentials", claimed Aditya, "in the history of human kind man has tried hard to know about the reality of life, may it be related to intra-personal, inter-personal, group behavior, concerned with either motivations or actual deeds, the urge to know – 'what can move a person to action?' "

"We have so many theories, so many explanations; yet, today we cannot say with certainty as to what is that universal thing that explains everything", said Param.

"We have got many explanations and many of them have proved correct and are of great use on many occasions, though not forever. Hitherto, these explanations have not exhausted our effort to find the one – perfect fit in all."

Something forced Sam to get involved in the assertions made by Aditya. "Do you really mean to propose a theory?" asked Sam, unbelievingly.

"I propose a theory before an esteemed audience of close friends, making them part of the history", laughed Aditya and continued, "I will endeavor to explain it now."

Aditya's serious deliberations forced them to get involved in the discussion, especially after the class on political thinkers, and Param asked, inquisitively, "Does that explain everything?"

"I am not sure, but how to understand human behaviour? Why people feel cheated by someone? And many other complex relations can be explained. It can even predict what could be the course of action to resolve the conflicts, the world facing today", claimed Aditya.

"Wow! It sounds interesting, but, why the name – potential?" asked Param.

"The word potential has got special relevance here. In electrical circuits current flows from higher potential to lower potential. It applies to the flow of water also that flows from higher altitude to lower, until external force is applied to stop or reverse it. Similarly, ideas and knowledge flow from those possessing more knowledge to those having less, or none at all, provided people have not put artificial barriers like prejudices and animosity, which stimulates them not to listen but fight. This can be found, if analyzed deeply, in every sphere of human interactions. For this reason lasting relationships are formed among people with potentials in different fields."

"Good! But, how is trade linked to it?" asked Parag.

"An individual buys from a person, who has something to sell, thus the flow of things or ideas are form a person, having more or surplus, to the one, who is deficient. Dearth of resource like currency or any other valuable commodity or thing, which is used as a barter acts as a barrier. Similar is the case of trade among countries; one country which has surplus, sales to the one which is deficient. We buy arms from the USA and sell textiles to it. However, if the buyer country were bankrupt then trade would not take place. To restart the trade one has to either remove the barrier or create more potential, by either earning or borrowing money, but borrowing is not sustainable as it creates a negative potential. This is evident in trade relations of countries, though in more complex form, and I won't burden you with my unpublished and unproved work."

"So that is how you explain why girlfriends walk away, especially Parag's girlfriend, who deserted him", commented Param that made everybody laugh.

"Yes dear Parag, you ought to have built your potential to remain in relation with her. Have no illusions in future. If you want someone to revere you eternally, then maintain greater potential, everlastingly", advised Aditya, igniting a burst of laughter.

"Is it that all the interactions among human beings happen due to difference in potential and barriers?" asked Parag.

"People meet, interact and exchange ideas till everyone has already shared whatever they knew and can't go further or some barrier prevents them from further deliberations. As in many meetings one says, 'I am leaving'. It is because either the person is bored or the barrier, like time, prevents him from extending the discussion. All the interactions, when analyzed deeply, reveal that there are only two principles at work whenever human beings interact – potential and barrier. If you understand this you can understand every other human being's behaviour."

"But, many theories already talk about such things. What is new about it?" said Parag interrupting the pace and containing the zeal with which Aditya was speaking. It could, however, not stop Aditya from putting across his understandings based on his unique experiences.

"Might be, but I conveyed my understanding of things in a crude form," he said in a low voice and continued, "this theory includes some other related fundamentals. One such fundamental is sustainability. Sustainability is a state of equilibrium where there is neither huge difference of potential nor much insulation to stop the flow of ideas. It is a stage where transactions seem to take place without hindrances, though the principles of difference of potentials operate in subtle manner. Things remain sustainable till one finds the commodity produced to be worth its salt. A country buys some commodity from USA, which in turn buys from

China and China buys from that country. However, if any link is broken, global imbalances and sudden depressions or peaks ensue. This explains why countries became slave to colonizing powers. Slave countries became slave because they had less physical and intellectual potential."

While other people sitting in the canteen chatted about the worldly affairs, these enlightened sages carried on with their deliberations, still not bored with many such lectures in the classes. "Can it explain our relations with Pakistan? " asked Neha.

"The theory of potential envisions, if Pakistan fails to get what it wants from India or if India fails to engage it, sensing the exhaustion of all its potential resources to influence India, Pakistan may resort to selling its nuclear weapons to the terrorists, to increase its bargaining power, clandestinely. It would simply increase it's potential to fight against India."

"Are you anti-Pakistan or a war monger", asked Neha.

"I am not against any country, as under such circumstances anyone would do this. It applies to any other country or agency or individual where immense power is concentrated in few selected hands without any accountability."

"I have another view on it", said Parag.

"What is that?" asked Param.

"If we become a global economic power, then Pakistan will not behave the way it does today", answered Parag.

"This is precisely what I am telling. Becoming economic power is nothing, but increasing the potential in an area, which is recognized by the whole world. And then any hostile country remains with only two options – either to interact in a meaningful way or still put a barrier and not interact at all. But, in both the cases it can't continue to wield it's negative influence", said Aditya.

"It may still try to be hostile, like North Korea to South Korea", objected Parag.

"May be, but, there too, North Korea remains only hostile and does nothing other than posturing to increase it's potential to remain relevant. Besides, don't forget that North Korea is a nuclear capable nation and has greater potential in this filed, though, South Korea counters this by fostering friendship with global giants and by being an economic powerhouse it has a greater overall potential", explained Aditya.

"That may be the reason for war, which is generally started by a party that considers itself to be equivalent or greater in potential", observed Neha at which Aditya said, "It is exactly what, this theory describes."

"Perhaps it is due to their faith or illusions in their abilities", said Parag.

"I am already bored with today's lecturer on Israel and Palestine and I am leaving now. See you guys", said Sam and left, while others just sat as if to prolong the discussion.

"How do you explain the relation between Israel and Palestine?" asked Neha, as if inclined to further enquire.

"The relation between Israel and Palestine is very complex as our professor tells. Can it really explain that?" asked Param excited with Aditya's ideas. He had once asked his professor, who could not give a conclusive answer.

"Not everything, but Israel builds its potential through violence in which it is superior so it has established its authority and is hard enough to be defeated. However, Palestine is weak, physically, on account of area, population and weaponry. But it continues to fight Israel physically, using violence as a means. No wonder it resultantly gets defeated every time or does not win at best. It fails to try increasing its potential in the sphere of non-violence. So it continues to sustain defeats. However, it strives to increase its potential through support from other countries, but the whole world is obsessed with their self-interest and are divided", described Aditya with his theoretical constructs, formed with his little experience of the world.

"I bet if Palestine use non-violence as a means to fight Israel patiently, it would eventually win. This is what Gandhi did, he increased the potential to fight against the British using non-violence as his weapon", said Neha.

"You are right. Palestine had tried non-violence once under the leadership of Yasser Arafat, won many supporters throughout the world, but not for long. Once the violence started again, they lost many of them."

"Can it explain Terrorism?" asked Param.

"Yes. Terrorism is a way of increasing potential. Whosoever has more potential or power wins in the end, or whosoever is more powerful at any given point of time, wins at that moment. If state has more power than the terrorist, it would win. In the modern world, generally, the power of the state is more so it wins most of the times otherwise becomes a failed state. A country like Afghanistan where terrorists, or non-state actors, had more power, won over the state and established their rule, which in turn forced her to seek outside help and increase her power to flush the terrorists out. This has been happening since ages, I am not stating anything new. It applies to other organizations or groups, as happened in the French Revolution where the bourgeois won over the King due to greater potential they had built over time."

They sipped coffee and extended their interesting discussion further. Now it was Aditya's turn to pose a question, drifting away a bit, he asked. "Can somebody explain the struggle between good and evil?"

"I can try to explain", replied Parag.

When other nodded to him to go ahead to explain he continued, "There is always a struggle going on between good and evil, vice and virtue. Sometimes, good wins and other times bad; however, whenever bad appears to win, the truth remains that good wins eventually, and then things begin again and the same game repeats. Good has more potential than evil, which may vary from time to time; this variance explains – why evil seems to be winning sometimes.

However, there is neither absolute beginning nor absolute end. Good is the inherent power of the world."

"Great! You seem to have mastered the understanding of this theory", said Aditya.

"Yes. May be, we will be ranked among great thinkers and writers", they laughed at this generous self-evaluation and Parag continued, "Today's world must attend to the social injustices taking place."

"There are so many thinkers and so many friends of the poor, yet life remains miserable for them. Who have made their lives so? Despite honest efforts, enlightening philosophies, and social theories, the deserving are denied justice; the workers crave for their rights", surmised Neha.

"You should present this theory before the world and then you need not study, as you would already be given doctorate in this theory", said Parag, teasingly.

"Do you think that people would listen to me? There have already seen so many theories. I do not wish to present a theory and become a boring academic genius. This is my understanding of the world, which I could not prevent from presenting before you. It may seem old wine in a new bottle. A new person meets with so many challenges and resistances that it requires immense potential to prove one's point"; said Aditya.

"Can this theory explain failures?" asked Param.

"People may fail due to various reasons, but they often fail for the want of efforts or because their competitor was better. It is a lesson that one should increase one's potential to win. One can increase one's potential in a variety of ways. Assume that a person is required to run hundred meters in ten seconds, to qualify for a tournament, and in trials scores eleven second, then that person should increase the potential to the extent till one clocks ten seconds", replied Aditya.

"Has your theory some more prescriptions?" said Parag, playfully.

"It has prescriptions that assist a person comprehend human relations and understand all kinds of transactions among people, societies and nations. It tells, build your potential, if you are losing. If you continue to strive, one day your potential could be unbeaten high. Always remember, those who are defeated are exposed to further attacks as they loose the potential, especially when they loose the potential suddenly; nevertheless, in such a situation one should not forget that potential could still be built. This is what ancient kingdoms did whenever they lost against a more powerful enemy, so did Britain, the USA achieved its remarkable success this way and China is doing now", said Aditya.

"Was this the reason that you preferred political science to science so that you become a thinker some day", said Param at which they laughed, "It is time for the next class", he reminded Aditya, who seemed to be unusually excited that they had never witnessed before. After finishing coffee they left for the afternoon class. They left the discussion there with a promise to continue it some other time, which never came.

□

16

At the start of second year in the college they had option to go for Himalayan Trekking expedition to Swargdwar in Uttrakhand, and they were required to submit their applications by the end of the month of June. The trek would commence in the first week of October. He gladly opted for it so did his best friends. They were greatly excited and submitted their requests the very day it was announced.

It was a lovely morning on which they were to leave for the much-awaited trek; the air was full of excitement, however, getting up to experience it and prepare to leave was arduous, as Aditya had partied with his friends the whole night and was asleep. Despite repeated protestations by Aditya, Parag had not listened and pushed him to bed. He got up, slothfully and unwillingly, and packed some pairs of clothes, jacket, trekking shoes, sleeping bag and a sheet to sleep on in the backpack, he also kept some medicine, goggles, sunscreen lotion, soap and other essential items. They packed all the things that were necessary for them as per the instructions of their guide, who would accompany them. They were given a set of walky-talky to be carried by the group leader and trailer.

"I hope you have kept all the important items suggested by the guide", he confirmed with Parag.

"Yes."

Twelve of them left New Delhi by a late night train that would reach them the next morning to Dehradun at about six o'clock. They reached the first destination and went to a hotel near the railway station; and after taking rest started for Sankri, which was their second destination for the day. They took the Garhwal Tourism Bus.

"How beautiful this route is, I feel on top of the world, said Sam sitting next to Aditya after they entered the serene Himalayas, leaving the plains much behind, surrounded by mountains from all the sides.

"Yes, I feel I am dreaming", replied Aditya.

"I have always thought of going to the Himalayas."

"I too have, and that is why it seems like a dream to me to be here. I was told that many people go to the Himalayas for salvation."

"It is always good to go on trekking expedition after a few years."

"You appear so confident about the trek in the beginning, it is better you reserve your views till we go back to our hostels."

"Yes provided you do not change sides and sit with Puja", mumbled Sam.

"How dare you think that? Will I leave a friend for a girl?" exploded Aditya.

"I was teasing you."

Parag laughed inviting everyone's attention, as he was sitting behind and listening to the interesting conversation, quietly.

After joining college, Puja had devoted herself completely to studies to fulfill her ambition. She was a kind of woman, who would hardly talk to people other than her close friend Neha. Aditya knew that people had a clue of what was transpiring between them for the past few days in the college canteen.

The whole journey was full of the beautiful mountains with green carpets of trees changing to pine form, as they scaled higher and higher. These mountains were divided in their pursuit by small rivulets that met later to become big rivers. The population became sparse as they crossed villages along the path towards higher mountains. Some mountains showed the sign of landslides that vastly occur during rains. It looked ugly amid the beauty of the pine forests and wild colourful flowers blooming at the top of some distant and higher mountains. They were still away from the snow-clad mountains, which appeared close from the windows of the bus, though were far away. The shops selling Maggie noodles, Parathas, packed chips and water were a common sight.

After the arduous journey by bus, meandering through the turns of the tortuous mountainous route, they reached Sankri at 3:00 in the afternoon.

They took lunch and had hardly relaxed when the guide ordered them, "start and reach Taluka, which is about ten kilometers away from Sankri". Taluka was the place where they would stay for the night. For next few days, in the Himalayas, they would trek for about ten to fourteen kilometers, would stay at forest guesthouses for the night before starting for a new destination every morning. This would continue till they climb Har-ki-doon and come back.

Their guide was a very sensible man, who gave them a sketch of the trekking route and allowed them their share of freedom and independence, desired immensely by the young Turks.

After a long journey by bus, they were tired, but were left with no other option than to walk to Taluka before sunset. They were warned that they couldn't take these mountain forests casually as they are full of snow leopards and bears, which are dangerous animals, however, it was fear that made them more perilous. Accordingly, they were advised to move in groups.

The forest appeared lonely, but was full of life. There were flowers of all hues, variety of trees, rivers, and birds. Each step was giving immense gratification to them, as they had never imagined that their wish to go to the Himalayas would ever be fulfilled with such vivid experience.

The group was enjoying the trek. People were chattering, experiencing and partaking the beauty of the mountains and forests, which they photographed and took to nature's invitation with delight. It was a unique experience for all of them, fit for saints to meditate. Some were still involved in their stupid worldly affairs – an affront to mother nature. Even the serenity and beauty of the Himalayas could not cast its spell on them. One thing was evident that everyone was happy.

Trekking is considered to be a big change over to the original man different from the worldly man of mundane pursuits. Trekking, apart from giving a sense of achievement, assists in discovering self and to face life squarely in all its ugliness and beauty, reality and romance, pleasure and pain.

We encounter lots of difficulties in life and often remain under duress due to insignificant things. It helps in understanding the universe and discovering the irrelevance of things, for which we continuously ruin our lives and forget significant things. It relieves all the stress and pressures.

At about 5 pm when they reached Taluka, the first destination. Being exhausted they dropped their belongings in the rooms and spread themselves on the floor. Aditya gathered some courage and came out of the room, sat on an elevated place and looked at a river flowing far away from them. His thoughts wandered with the wings of imagination,

"A directionless river, cutting mountains, rushing through deep alleys, has fallen so deep that no trace of coming back is visible. It is forced to fall through the narrow path along the mountains. It is running like a drifter. This nascent river can be compared to a life running directionless. This forgetful life is so lost that there is no one to listen to its sound, to see it's flexing, which could have given it a feeling of self-importance.

The darkness of deep water carrying forgotten shadows, the shadows carrying the memory of lost days, memories seem so lovely, only when they are lost, the lost world and no echoes are heard for so long,

Such is the depth immeasurable. So desperate yet so helpless,

So zealous yet without accomplishments,

So successful yet so alone."

He came back and saw others, who were already lying like crocodiles – breathless on a sunny sand beach. They slept like dogs and woke up only to the call of dinner bells from outside and discovered that it was already 9 pm. They could not believe that they were so vastly fatigued. To their surprise they found that the dinner was arranged near a bonfire. After finishing the dinner and talking about the journey, slumberously, they went back to sleep on the orders of the guide – to start at 8 o'clock in the morning.

* * *

Sun was setting over the top of the mountains. Between two peaks was a tiny pass from which this river was entering into the small valley in Taluka: it was a beautiful natural delight. Looking at the splendid sight of the day, which was meeting the dusk unilaterally, they had decided to reach near the tiny beautiful river, which was visible at a moderate distance from their place of stay, the forest rest house, early next morning when the sun would peep through the gorge which separated the two mountains and provided passage to the river to flow by.

As decided Aditya, Param, Sam and Puja got up at 6 am and left for the adventure.

"It was a terrific night", said Param.

"Why", asked Sam, while Puja looked at Aditya.

"Because fearing the snow leopard I could not venture out to ease myself in the night." They laughed at this candid but facetious acceptance.

"But, snow leopards are not normally found here."

Param barely realized that he misunderstood the situation.

"We will have to be back before half past seven, as the guide expected us to start for Osla at 8 o'clock."

"Do not worry dear Param, we will certainly be back by 7:30 am. I have already packed my belongings and I guess all of us must have finished our morning duties", quipped Aditya, who wanted not to spoil his mood on such unnecessary tensions.

Puja did not care what transpired between others while they were on their way to the small river. She was lost in the romantic beauty of the Himalayas at dawn. She glanced at the colours in the sky that started shifting, beginning with grey and continuing from blue to green then to orange and to yellow, finally, ending up in the black mountains. She was completely hypnotized by the beauty of the Himalayas.

Aditya looked at her and realized how content and happy she was; it gave him great happiness. While others kept on walking towards the river; something was happening between them.

They hardly believed their eyes when they reached the river. It was much bigger than what it appeared from the rest house. The music of swirling river through rocky terrain was so enchanting that one hardly felt like leaving the sight. The river was not only big, but was deep as well. They desisted from crossing the river after assessing the depth of the river. Besides, the effusion was such that it could sweep anything coming in its way. They learned a lesson – it is difficult to judge things from a distant place in the mountains.

They sat near the water on separate rocks, threw stones in the water with a soft plop, creating ripples on the surface and tried to make them float. They felt a sense of achievement when the stone touched the ripples as many times as possible before getting disappeared into the current.

The water in the river was so clear that one could even see the small stone and pebbles resting at the bottom of the river. The river gushed through rocks and made its way to distant places. It was soothing and peaceful and after listening to it anybody could relapse into deep meditation. There existed such harmony that one could believe that time had stopped. Nobody had imagined that such a beautiful world existed in the abode of the Himalayas, which appear more vulnerable every time one looks at the devastation brought by rains and landslides.

The discourse continued between Param and Sam that meant nothing for Aditya and Puja, who were lost in their own world. It was a dream for both of them to be in the romantic Himalayas someday – alone, not knowing that they could be so thinly populated, and trekking there could be so difficult. He had read that Himalayas have many great pilgrims like Kailas-Mansarovar, Kedarnath, Badrinath, Yamunotri, and Gangotri and many lesser destinations. Many important rivers of the country have their births in the Himalayas and have watered northern India and blessed it with various prosperities. These rivers are the lifeline not only of India but also of China, Pakistan and Bangladesh and some other countries. Therefore, it was almost a pilgrimage for him, hardly religious, but more spiritual.

The Himalayas, a godly place, are a perpetual source of knowledge and wisdom and saints come here to acquire wisdom, salvation and spiritual strength in the blessed solitude.

Puja was sitting silently on a rock not far away from Aditya.

At 7:10 am when someone interrupted them.

"Hey guys its time to move. If we get late they would look for us as lost."

"Don't worry, I have told Neha that we are going to the river and will be back by 7:45 am", replied Puja, surprising everybody.

Then they trudged back to the rest house where they found others taking breakfast. Hungry as they were, they joined.

They started for Osla from Taluka at 8:30 am.

Puja walked along with Aditya for the whole day, hardly speaking, but there was something on her mind that did not come out. He tried to make conversation, but did not succeed and the entire day was spent looking at the scenic beauty. It was like a dream. With Puja he could not go beyond academic discussions. Frustrated with his own inability, he decided to keep silent. Once she felt jealous when she had seen Maya interacting with Aditya in the class. Maya was a beautiful girl and Puja had noticed that Maya was taking extraordinary interest in him, though only Aditya knew that their discussions were purely academic. It was heartening that Puja was aware of it; it made him feel happy.

They reached Osla at around 3 pm after walking for about eleven kilometers.

Some slept, some played cards and some chatted and discussed about the route and the beauty of the Himalayas while some others went for a walk. There was as small group of drinkers, led by Raghav that enjoyed the liquor he had brought. Four of them were always together and it was this common interest that kept them in league, till the end, not only during the trekking, but also throughout their college life.

After dinner they went to bed with the instructions to start for Har-ki-doon the next morning at 8 o'clock. This time they were told specifically to start on time, as it was twelve kilometers away and the route was very steep. Besides, the trek would now involve heights of fifteen thousand feet and above, and it rains almost every day at such high altitudes.

Two hours passed after midnight when Raghav cried, "Help, somebody help! It is snake there!"

The cry woke up everyone.

"Where is the snake?" asked one friend, who was sleeping besides him.

"Under my sleeping bag."

"It is not there", confirmed his friend after search.

"Then it might be inside the sleeping bag."

"You always drink and turn the world topsy-turvy. For God's sake stop behaving like this", said his roommate, who was fed up with his drunken fits.

They looked everywhere, but they could not find the snake.

"It was a rat I believe, look at the top of the table where a rat is still eating the left over".

Everyone laughed and went back to sleep; some of them cursed him.

□

17

It was 8 O'clock when everybody was ready with full trekking gears. They took breakfast and started the march towards their final destination – Har-ki-doon.

Puja left a little early. Aditya was left with Parag, for they were the last ones to start. There was a river running along with their route. It was a constant companion. However, this river too was lost after seven kilometers of the journey. But now Puja was back. She was perched on a rock in the small stream near a dhaba that was situated a little above the stream. It was serving Maggie to the customers. Puja was sitting silently, and offered Maggie to Aditya, when he reached and sat next to her. He looked back for Parag, who was nowhere near. He had sense enough when to leave two people alone.

They were almost the last ones in the group; they ate and looked at the mountains. There were only few houses with people sitting on the threshold.

"What drives these people to live here in such isolated places?" asked Puja.

"I think people live here because of peace, love of nature, and attachment with the native land", replied Aditya.

"You might be right, but I feel it is the habit of living that makes them live here".

"Given a chance would you like to live here?" he questioned.

"Yes, occasional but not forever".

"Don't you think these solitary, imposing mountains provide the best opportunities for meditation and food for thought".

"I agree with you."

It seemed he was reading her thoughts. Though, she did not respond, she looked directly into his eyes. He also knew that she agreed; but her feminine coyness came in her way. This silence was a source of great worry for him. He wanted to carry the discussion beyond nature and their individual beliefs, but he struggled. Puja was normal in her manners and calm outside, but was agitated deep down within, like the river they saw yesterday, this calm was bothering him. May be it was the last chance for him to express his feelings for her.

"We are left behind, and now there is no one to show us the way."

"You should not worry. Raghav is always there to bank on. He always lags behind and today the guide is also accompanying him."

"May be he has failed to understand me this time also", she thought.

They walked for three more kilometers; now only two kilometers remained for them to reach their final destination; the ascent was difficult and she was too tired to walk.

"Give me your Bag pack", he asked.

Initially she protested, but finally gave up, for she did not have energy to carry the bag; she took it back after she was comfortable.

"What do you want to prove?" he asked, being upset on returning the bag.

"Nothing?" she replied, aggressively.

He knew that she was the kind of a girl, who would not like to incur unnecessary obligations.

"I feel that everyone is selfish and I think there is nothing bad about it", he said.

"What made you say this?"

"I wanted to change the topic, as you did not allow me to help you carry your luggage." She laughed while he continued, "everyone lives for himself and for nobody else. However, people find it difficult to accept."

"Will you explain what do you mean?"

"I thought about many relations and passed them through the filter of selfishness, and found that no act was absolutely selfless. Gandhiji worked for people, but he never claimed himself to be altruistic. Whatever he did was for his individual satisfaction, it gave him contentment and he did not want to impress anyone. He never thought that people would be happy if he did this or that. He never asked anybody to follow him forcefully, but people followed him because of their own selfishness. It was selfishness that brought people close to him. If he was not acceptable to people, they would never have followed him, as they did to so many others, as people always do. Selfishness brought the best out of him and did so much good to the society. It is better for us to be selfish. We serve the society better when we are selfish", he said, being disgruntled with her conduct.

"But some people claim that if we become selfish the whole world would turn evil and nobody would help people in distress and there would be chaos."

"It is assumed but is not correct. There are people who get satisfaction by being kind to others with selfless work that motivates them to be social or benevolent. People, who help one, can help anyone. They are not selective in their efforts, as you must have observed people helping the accident victims; it is this spirit that augments their happiness. Selfishness is good, but is hardly viewed as a good thing by the society. People, scarcely realize that selfishness is selfishness, it is neither good nor bad.

On the other hand, there could be an evil man, who would kill someone to earn money. He would be hated and termed as selfish. In contrast to him there could be a person, who might help someone in need, yet will not be called selfish. But the fact is that both are selfish as they strive for satisfaction."

"Then you would say our parents are also selfish, who have given us birth", she alleged, uncomfortably, but soon got her composure back.

"Yes, but do not misunderstand me. Our parents never thought of bringing us in this life for the benefit of the society, but for them. It provided them satisfaction, delight of playing with us and a security for old age."

"It is pathetic. I can't think of it anymore. Please stop it."

"No. It is not. Selfishness is not bad per se. Please open your mind then you will appreciate it", he requested and continued to persuade her with his arguments.

"Our minds are so engraved and prejudiced with good and evil that we define everything in those two terms. Is it not selfishness that whatever fits in one's favourable beliefs, becomes selfless, and whatever not, becomes selfish? The world would still remain, what it is today, if we accepted the fact that we are inherently selfish, we would have good and bad people then also and the world would not come to an end. By this we would not befool ourselves, and we would never resort to lying – 'We are for the society.' Were Newton not selfish, had he listened to his mom or dad, we might still be waiting for a selfish man to discover gravity. If Einstein were not selfish we would not have got the theory of relativity, and so many other things that made the world a better place to live. It became possible to discover innumerable things because the discoverer or inventor was selfish in his approach, though he might have neglected many things and made his families and relatives unhappy by being so."

"Do you mean to say that you are selfish ", she asked, worried by his extreme thoughts.

"Yes, by accepting the truth I can contribute to the society in a better way without pretending to be selfless. It would be without the burden of failing to act for what I intended to do, than doing something people wanted and desired from me for their happiness. I too am selfish, for I intend to do that work, which gives me immense satisfaction and bliss. If anything is forced on me then I would pretend that I am doing good, would get my photographs clicked for newspapers, to show-off and for self deception, with no sincerity and honesty."

"I see."

"Every individual has two mental frames. You too must have heard of the real self and the ideal self, described by the psychologists."

"Yes, I have, but how they relate to selfishness?"

"The real self is made by the actual life experiences and desires of a person. Whereas, ideal self is made of what is prescribed to a person to be right, which many a times, is not practiced by the person himself preaching it to the others. Those traits or habits, which are practiced, become part of the real self, whereas theoretical constructs that are taught or prescribed become part of the ideal self, for example, 'one should help others.' If a person practices what he teaches to his kid, then it becomes part of both the real and ideal self, whereas, if he teaches one thing and practices the other then the ideal self gets differentiated from the real self, and distortions follow."

"But, some habits which are practiced can still not become part of the real self."

"Yes, it can happen due to various other experiences and factors. Influenced by the ideal self or introspection or the unique experiences of life, one may find stealing to be bad even when one observes people stealing. Whatever we do is determined by these two factors. Those who can understand these two facets of an individual can predict about his behaviour under a particular circumstance, and can do wonders."

"How do you explain people returning the lost valuables found on road or elsewhere then?" she reasoned.

"Let us assume that there are two persons walking on a lonely road. The person walking behind sees a hundred rupee currency note fall from the pocket of another person, he may keep it, if his real self prompts him and dominates over the ideal self."

"But many people may return it", she argued with some pain.

"If the ideal self dominates in that person, and still he keeps it, then he would be punished with guilt by his conscience. To save oneself from such contrition, the person avoids keeping the currency note and returns it, and in turn, gets rewarded by the ideal self that he did the right thing and performed as taught to him or as he perceived to be correct, which brings him lots of satisfaction."

We live only for contentment and joyfulness. We sometimes act ethically and some other times immorally, yet we always act as per either of these two constructs and thus, society will remain both benevolent and evil. However, those who have similar ideal and real self achieve the kind of personality like Gandhi, Lincoln, Mandela, and Mother Teresa had. Such people achieve self-actualization, which is a source of perpetual bliss.

"I still cannot go with most of the things you said", she said after questioning and listening, vastly, on the issue she hardly agreed with.

"At least with some", he laughed and continued, "People think that they should be altruists and yet they act selfishly. This becomes a great reason for their misery, sorrow and discontentment, for there is constant struggle between real and ideal selves. Those who know that they are selfish are similar to the people who find no difference between the ideal and the real self."

"I learned that people have self-interests more than anything else. Even truth does not matter before self-interests. Anyway, what is more important to you? Your career or me?" she asked, being puzzled and visibly disturbed, interrupting him, after inferring his feelings, which took him by surprise.

"Was it in any way an acceptance of love for him?" his heart questioned his mind. Believing that, he replied, without getting deprived of a last probable chance to express himself, "My first love is my dream with you included. It is an inclusive thing. Honestly, I would expect the same from you also." Without saying so many things he answered many questions in one shot that were lingering in her mind. He expected a reply that was not forthcoming. She was committed to her goal in life and felt that someday it might come in conflict with her personal life.

* * *

At a point near the top of a hill while following the path towards Har-ki-doon, Aditya felt that perhaps his whole life might not offer him the ecstasy he was experiencing. He was with Puja on the top of a cliff; they were resting for a while, the sky was blue with some whitish grey clouds, which were sailing over the peaks of mountaintops far way; some mountains were dark green with a blanket of pine trees everywhere, some others were totally white covered with snow. A river far away still divided the mountains into two halves. An intense reflection from the snow obliterated the sight of these mountains.

They started again after taking some rest, and finally reached their destination – Swargdwar (Har-ki-doon). According to the legends it is the place from where Pandava's, as mentioned in the Mahabharata reached heaven directly. It started raining when they entered inside the two-roomed forest rest house, as if clouds waited for their arrival. They had reached a height of sixteen thousand feet. Everybody looked contented. Puja collapsed in bed alongside Neha, who had reached an hour earlier. Aditya joined Parag, who meaningfully grinned at him. He was happy for Aditya and had a plan ready to extend the adventure.

He told Aditya, "Let us go to the hill in front of us. We will climb it to outdo others in scaling little higher than our group."

"But, it is too steep and high."

"We will scale it only partially."

Aditya knew his friend was glutted with strange ideas. He agreed without contestation. Both took GPS cum altimeter and left for the hill after the rain stopped; Puja was watching them leave from the window. She admired his drive and passion, she was tired and first gazed at the mountain he was climbing.

Both of them sat for about half an hour at a height of seventeen thousand feet, as if celebrating their remarkable achievement. They could see a small river, which was forced to fall along the narrow path, flowing its way between huge mountains. It was running like a drifter; it were so lost that there was no one to listen to its sound; to see it's flexing, which could have given it a feeling of self-importance. Strange was its journey; it flowed sleeplessly, gurgled, kissed the rocks, air, and trees. It strived unsuccessfully to fly, but the shear burden of its weight brought it back to the land, this effort, however, didn't go waste, it impressed many hearts and provided a source of inspiration.

They returned back, when the twilight was embracing the sky with a unique sense of wonderful achievement evident in their sparkling eyes. Nothing can be compared with the ultimate feeling of bliss derived from scaling a peak higher than others. Perhaps, people scale Mount Everest for this pleasure, when they risk their lives for this delightful competitive feeling of winning over one's limitations.

They were to stay at Har-ki-doon for the night. Since Puja was part of this expedition, it was difficult to tell whether Aditya opted for the expedition because of her or for sheer excitement of trekking the Himalayas. After taking the evening tea, he was sitting a little away, in front of the rest house, while others were inside taking rest. While gazing at the snow-clad mountains, he thought he was entering into a dream.

When others came out and were chatting he was sitting in front of her. She looked gorgeous and graceful with Himalayan peaks in the background; the mountains were snow-covered, some blackish green with pine forest in the front. She looked as graceful as Himalayas – love transforms everything.

He wondered who was more beautiful, the face he saw in front of him or the Himalayas forming the background of that stunning countenance. This ineffable beauty was indeed like Himalayan peaks, which appear very near, clearly visible, yet remain far away when one approaches it. They recede even farther when one tries to approach them; it was an unimaginable and expensive luxury. He wondered whether it was a myth or a reality or a creation of his own mind from the reflections of the past.

She aroused both hope and despair. Her magnificence was irresistible. Her rosy cheeks, soft nose, small pink lips and long tresses were romantically defined. They were embracing her and engulfing others in a black fog of imagination. She was looking at him. He was entering into a new dream. Her alluring looks could drive anyone crazy.

"Now life would be unbearable without her even for a day, if she was not seen amid the clouds of destiny", thought Aditya.

There were fleck of snow showering softly on his head and she was growing indistinct with the haze. She was gone and what he saw in front of him was another Himalayan beauty, one of the several unknown peaks of Himalayas. When he awoke from sleep and retrieved his senses he realized that it was a dream. Great dream to be sure, uniting their beings. A fog of love was in the air.

Himalayas are incredibly beautiful, even the most phlegmatic could fall for them. They can drive anyone mad. Love lingers even when you leave them, that's how they seduce people with their captivating charm. Such is the romance of Himalayas and such is the beauty of Himalayas.

* * *

Next morning they started the return journey to Sankri. The guide Gopal told them that the journey back was towards downhill, thus it would not take long to reach back to Sankri, still they would take a break at Taluka and would go to Sankri the next day, from where they would take a bus, to return back to Dehradun, as they had to catch the late night train to Delhi. It was a very tight schedule for them from now on. In two days they would cover difficult terrain and catch the train.

On the journey back to Taluka, Puja and Aditya were together again. He was uncomfortable; the situation was growing tense as he tried to suppress his emotions, especially when Puja was around. They talked a lot on their way back and he, inadvertently, told her that he wanted to become a politician; shë was very uncomfortable.

They were nearing Taluka, Puja unexpectedly asked him, "do you really like me?" taking him by surprise. He replied, "Yes, I do, or else why should I be with you for so long? Can't you feel it? How many times will I need to tell you, dear?" An emboldened Aditya made things clear.

"Is it just liking or something more than that?"

"It is more than that, it is love – the deepest affection I have for you. The depth of my soul is filled with love, ever since we met. I have been living in a world, which is neither real nor unreal; I daydream about you and fantasize about you. I do not call it desperation, but I am always in hurry to share my feelings with you".

"Were you afraid of something?"

"Yes, but does it matter".

"Yes it matters, for there is no fear and favour in love".

"But do you like me".

"You claim that you know me and that is the reason you love me, yet you can't understand that I would never talk to a person so much, whom I dislike. Yes, I like you and I love you from the bottom of my heart. I liked you the day I met you first time in the train."

"I have never felt talking to any girl so satisfying like I feel with you."

"Do not lie, I have seen you flirting with Maya in the class, they laughed while she continued, "do you think that I am a kind of girl who would accept a proposal so easily."

"Why have you taken so long to accept it? You have made me suffer profoundly, though you cherished every feeling and thought I had for you", the world around Aditya changed as he pronounced this.

They looked at each other exchanging glances, while their souls met. Suddenly the world around them grew romantic and the mountains burst with beautiful wild flowers, which appeared more vibrant on the mountaintop. He was rapturous as if he had achieved salvation in his life, as if it was raining and he was dancing in it, as if he was at the top of the Mount Everest, as if he chose to be there for this magic. Words failed to explain his feelings and when he was about to say something, she stopped him from uttering another word, as their lips were locked in a pure union. He held her close to his bosom. Her tresses covered his face. The snow-clad mountains, rivers, flowers and sky watched the spectacle of their love. Far away at the horizon the earth was kissing the sky as if celebrating their romance. Both had their hands together when they reached Taluka.

The next day they started for Sankri from where they were supposed to take the bus to Dehradun. They reached Dehradun at 10 pm. They were not late for the train. It would start at a little before midnight. They sat on the railway platform waiting for the train, boarded the train and went to sleep when the train arrived at the platform silently.

* * *

Once back to Delhi, Aditya was in his hostel's room reconciling the reality with the dream. He had woken from a beautiful dream. He asked his friend and roommate Parag, "Is it real or I was dreaming about the Himalayan Trek".

"It is real, my dear, but you have to tell whether your friendship with Puja is meaningful?" who had no doubt about what transpired between them at a height of sixteen thousand feet.

Both of them laughed while Parag hugged him and said, "So finally she consented?"

"I did not put any proposal. Yes, we are in a deep relationship."

□

18

Exams for the last year were approaching and students were already planning for their future. Aditya, had the only raison d'être that was to join politics after completing the college education, while his father wanted him to become a civil judge. He wanted to be a lawyer when he was in school, but later decided to lead people by pursuing his career in politics. The mock drill of politics in the college had given him ideas, and to become a lawyer was only an option. However, his friends were already looking and preparing for career in management, bureaucracy, law, media and so on.

The journey to enter any of these fields was, however, not so easy, as it required excellent performance in competitive entrance examinations. He was not sure of his success in the field of politics, but his passion, courage and belief in his abilities along with the inspiring words of his mother pushed him to act and to achieve something singular in life, something that fills him with contentment as a self imposed ambition.

Only a day was left for the exam to begin. The canteen looked deserted and Parag was as usual enjoying coffee.

"Hey, you are here! Why did you not tell me that you were coming here", said Parag, he pulled a chair and ordered a coffee.

He offered snacks to Aditya while they talked about college friends and the career they had close to their hearts.

Aditya, who was quiet so far, decided to share his inner thoughts with him that he had shared only with Puja.

"I have decided to join politics and work for the people, immediately after leaving the college, for it would satisfy my desires and dreams", said Aditya.

Parag was surprised and it took him a moment to say something. "You can be a politician alright, but to win elections one has to be rich, as millions of rupees are required to contest elections. Besides, one has to have a reputation of a crook, whom people fear, for fear is the eventual motivator. Only after these qualifications one can think of winning elections in India. Democracy has different connotations in different parts of the world. In this part it is synonymous with money, muscle power, caste, class, religion and corruption. Without being corrupt, monetarily, one can't be rich – the first requisite to win elections. Without money it is suicidal to fight elections? Those who contest extract money from the businessmen, ideologically committed local people and the corrupt local government officials from whom the politicians usually demand share from their illegitimate earnings from the money meant for development."

Aditya replied, "Come what may, I am determined to take a plunge into politics, which is my sole aim in life. I agree with you that winning election requires immense efforts, but I want to prove that it is possible to achieve one's dreams, howsoever challenging, they might appear. The future holds promise for the educated and spirited youth like us. It is my conviction and I hope people will support me and many more like me."

"Well, I appreciate and respect your decision. "

"What about your CAT results?"

"It will be announced today!"

"When?"

"In the evening. But it is my wish that you first complete your law degree."

"Yes, dear, I have decided to join law in south campus."

They talked for better part of an hour and when Aditya left telling him that he had some important work, Parag knew what was that 'important work'; his mind was filled with ambitious thoughts.

* * *

Puja always fought with Aditya over his choice of career. She wanted to get into the IAS and wanted Aditya to tow her line. Though she knew that to suggest so would mean disturbing their relationship. She informed him, "I have applied for admission in JNU, and within a month the entrance and admission process would be over" and asked a futile question, "why don't you join me?"

"I have decided to try my luck in the arena of politics. Though, I will join law for masters as a part time student, but my main thrust would be politics." He once again confirmed her.

She could not control her emotions, and out of her desperation to convince Aditya to pursue a different career said, "Why you always think of joining politics? Are you a power monger?" though she forgot in her desperation that she too wanted to become an IAS officer for power with a security of job.

Sensing her mood, he pulled the discussion in another direction, instead of fighting over her remark, he replied, "Yes, I want power, not for self aggrandizement, but for my happiness, for I love to work for others."

"Why are you after power? Life, without it, can still be beautiful."

"People bow to power. Powerful must establish that their power is unchallengeable in the specific sphere. The best example is international relations in which countries make friends if they feel that the opponent is more powerful and fights if they have doubt that they are comparable. It gets very complex as we analyze it from this angle."

"Now don't start a lecture on Political Science. I have had enough of it."

"Its you who have started this. Have you not chosen your career for the same reason?"

"People should learn from you how to change the subject."

While they strolled around the college campus Aditya continued, "America is an example. The emergence of China is another; every country including Pakistan is respecting it because it has established its hegemony. On the other hand, since India's hegemony is not established, she is opposed by Pakistan and few other nations, vociferously, in international fora. Both believe that they are comparable and can finish each other. However, after its nuclear tests Pakistan feels equal in strategic sphere."

Getting engrossed in the discussion she asked, "Is power always aggressive?"

"Power does not only mean brute physical power, it could be anything that has the strength to establish the authority of the power holder, like democracy in which universal suffrage gives great power into the hands of the powerless, poor and downtrodden. They can topple a government – such is the power of democracy. Thus, weapon of peace or non-violence could be used to establish authority."

"The way Gandhi established his authority!"

"Gandhi used peaceful techniques and love as a weapon against violence and hate. He won over his enemies and rivals using a different weapon, the weapon of Non-Violence. His weapon was stronger than violence during his time because he knew the nature of Indian People and their faith in peaceful coexistence. Indians could have never won against physically superior British forces using violence unlike the bloody revolutions that happened in France or Russia. Besides, he knew that if violence was used against British, who had mastered in war and weapons and modern technology, would quell such violent resistance, as they did during many mutinies, especially in 1857."

"Do you mean to say Gandhi used non-violence because he knew that he could not have won against the mighty British with violence?" asked a puzzled Puja.

"Yes. And do you think his techniques could have worked in the medieval times? No. He was intelligent enough to understand the power of people and media in a democracy like Britain. People had already seen enough violence and were tired of war, thus, non-violence mattered. He knew that using his weapons of peace, he could force the British government to grant independence. You can find a similar fact in Martin Luther King's struggle in America. He also used civil disobedience and you know the results."

"All right, I agree you are better suited for the choice you have made."

"You or my career?" asked Aditya at which she smirked.

It lifted her somber mood and they decided never to interfere with each other's professional choices, which remained the mainstay of their relationship. Such professional choices require different strategies and planning, which meant different paths for them. They decided to watch a movie, perhaps, before they met for the last time.

They reached PVR Priya, bought tickets. The movie was about to end when he realized that his hand was locked in hers, perhaps she too was not aware of it. He felt the warmth of those beautiful hands. Both looked at each other for a while not contesting the different goals and dreams they had in life, 'Who would ask for the sacrifice?' They were present physically in the theatre, watching movie, though their thoughts were venturing elsewhere. After the movie, his mind was constantly thinking about the impending separation.

"How will you feed yourself?"

"I will take some part time job, may be at some call center."

"You know how tough it would be for a man like you. Don't you want to reconsider?"

"Can we not be together again", asked Aditya ignoring her question.

"You have to decide", replied Puja.

"I love to be always with you, but I never mean to create any trouble in your professional life."

"Once you had told me that everything we do have selfishness behind it. I thought over it and concluded that love is the answer for all of our problems. It fills us with bliss. It is love that brought us together. Selfishness can make us successful, whereas love provides contentment. I know I love you as much as you do, but that does not mean I should come in your way."

They did not like to make an issue out of the situation, for it would mean betrayal of the values on which their relationship prospered. They reached her hostel. Overwhelmed with the thoughts of separation, she kissed him while he embraced her holding warmly in his strong arms and was in no mood to leave her. With the excitement over, he dropped her in the hostel. She stood there with her eyes welled up with tears. He also looked back, but had difficulty in hiding his tears, which were infecting the very air with emotions. They would leave after the exams forever – what would be the fate of their relationship – they knew not.

After the results were announced most of the students had already left the campus. Parag got admission in IIM Ahmedabad; Puja joined JNU and Aditya joined south campus to study Law.

When these friends were leaving college, Parag asked his friends, "Will we meet again? We should continue to meet." A disoriented Aditya replied in a sultry tone, "No". Hearing this there were altercations between Parag and Aditya. Parag believed in the spirit of friendship and never expected to hear this from Aditya, who was his best friend.

Sam assured an emotionally agitated Parag. They promised to meet as often as possible and shall always be in effective terms.

* * *

It was the day when relationship was at stake. Some encounters during the college life could not to be forgotten; the one with Puja was definitely not there. Both were leaving without any commitment for the future. They needed a slight expression of sacrifice to be together in life, but they believed that love couldn't be monopolized, so none of them expressed it.

The end of college life and the youth was bullying Aditya to the discomfort of another new life. While, he walked across those beautiful jungles, down the paths of loneliness on a distant land, flowers were blooming amidst the thorns of the ugly plants like his comforts and discomforts. The spring of those days had some chill about them. The fear of losing someone very close distressed him, in the winter of love. The thoughts were interwoven, to appear as innocent and as weak, as a wild creeper taking shelter on a dry eucalyptus. His loneliness was shared by the river coiled across the landscape, and the thoughts by the whirlpool inside the water looking so calm from above as he once saw in the Himalayas. Yet, he kept on walking those memory lanes to peep into the glimpses of the faded past.

She disappeared from his view; sms and mobile amid repeated rings, which were the only source to remain in touch with her. She had the capacity to drive anyone crazy and he was no exception. As the vivid imagination took the form of reality, the soul woke up from the dream. How strange is the world? The wheel of time runs without waiting for anyone, things change leaving only the memories behind. With the flux of time, relations change so fast. Only a few days back the world looked very familiar, but now everything had vanished. The world of reality is as emotionless as the space above the sky.

The heart churns dreams to be either destroyed or accomplished. Many questions, many answers and many explanations that were still lingering in the mind had found no vent. Life was once again at the crossroads of fortunes painting the memories with the colours of hope. Which brush would destiny choose and what colours the life would prefer no one could guess.

□

19

Aditya moved on to chase his dreams. He forgot everything in his quest and endeavours to excel in life. There is no greater pleasure than chasing and realizing one's dream. The struggle to achieve one's most important goal in life is more gratifying and memorable than realizing the goal, which seems dwarf before determinations.

While he was in Delhi, he met Puja once, after which he could hardly meet her, as she remained busy with her committed pursuit; likewise he too had become occupied with his life. He changed his mobile number so that all contacts were barred and even though Puja tried to establish contact, he avoided her, for he did not like her to distract her from her cherished dream. If you really love someone and care for her, sacrifices has to be made, he made it gladly. However, both suffered.

He tried to get elected as a Councilor, but did not succeed and later when he tried his luck in assembly polls, he failed there too. However, he achieved one thing – his law degree. He left Delhi after three years and came to Bhopal to pursue his dream in a different way, despite the advice and persuasions of his friends, relatives and well wishers, for to become a politician and win election in India one requires a lot of money, cunningness and practical outlook – the three things he did not possess. He listened to his inner self and ignored them, as he believed that the pleasure of life is not in walking a dictated path, instead it lies in suffering while chasing one's own dreams. Life without chasing dreams and ideals is an empty life where there is no refreshing breeze, no fragrance emitting flowers, no starry sky and no hope of the rising sun.

His sufferings had no end, though he had waded through difficulties single mindedly so far, yet he felt dejected. He suffered his defeats alone and did not involve his parents in his fortunes. He did not succumb to temporary setbacks and adversities and stood his ground. He was ready to take up even an ordinary job than surrender to defeat, for it did not chime with his character. He contemplated to find answers, meditating on infinity with irresistible tears and crushed dreams. His spirit was wounded, but not the passion, to seek the cherished goals. He thought, "is this a punishment for following one's dream?" but he remembered the verse of an Urdu poet, who refused to believe that in the pitch darkness of life there wouldn't be a moon to guide him to his destination.

The poor and indignant sitting huddled together, receiving warmth from each other's body made even hunger to laugh; nobody knows where in such harsh winter birds go. The long unending winter was ruthless. His world was lost in the noon shine, the dismal gloom during the daylight; yet, his life was devoid of bright sunshine; a life trying to free itself from the shackles of an unknown fear, so slow amidst fast changing times; a life that is alone even in the midst of oceans of people. Yet, such a life could be an inspiration for many, so strange is the world, inspiration from the depth of a hollow soul.

The winter's dismal setting engulfed his mind. His failures did not dishearten him; on the contrary they further strengthened his resolve. The self-immolating phoenix rises young and strong from his ashes.

"A long absence from home would be amply compensated by a homecoming that would rejuvenate me", he thought and left for his home – parents on such occasions are of great help. Coincidentally, Danny also came to attend a wedding in the town; Danny gave him a call to meet.

He often went to the top of the beautiful Hill of Devi, whenever he returned to his home in Dewas. This place, nostalgically, gave him lots of relief. Sitting there, he pondered, "Oh! Devi, the power of the universe, what is my fault – is it that a downtrodden has chosen to enrich his dreams to carve out his destiny? I am a broke, what would I offer you apart from my tears and sorrow, which I have, in abundance."

He was with Danny; they talked about their school friends, where had they settled and what they were doing.

"Where are you these days?"

"I am in Chennai working in a multinational company as a software engineer."

"What about you?"

"I have completed law and shall soon start legal practice in Bhopal District Court, besides continuing my struggle in politics."

Hearing this, long back, Danny had felt uncomfortable, he still felt uneasy at his resolve, but now maturity donned him.

Danny had recently met Arpita. He told him, "She is divorced. She was devastated after divorce, but she has reconciled with her life and is now doing well. The only difference I could make out, when I met her recently, was that she has become a chain smoker." While Danny spoke Aditya was elsewhere.

Arpita loved Aakash and spent fabulous time together. Promises and no artificial boundaries to separate them, their parents approved their relationship and they got married after a long courtship. As they lived closer, got closer and closer, till a sudden shock rocked their dreams, the world tumbled, and the earth gaped menacingly. The shock of closeness was felt too late. The passion of love was difficult to douse, but its warmth was felt for too long. She was aghast with Aakash's attitude that drove her into the darkness; he touched the rock bottom of her heart. Relationship was torn apart by a chasm—an insurmountable one.

The soul was lost, the identity destroyed and a permanent vacuum was created in her heart. The soul however, survived the onslaught and shoved her to regain the lost hopeful promising horizon. Her spirit withstood the winters of her life and she started building her life from the scratch. Such spirit could be idolized in a temple and worshipped by a destitute.

"Oh! Sir where are you lost?" interjected Danny and forced him to come back from his enigmatic reflections. They came down back to the town.

Danny left the next day inviting Aditya to visit Chennai and promised to be in touch.

* * *

Another evening he was sitting, being forlorn, at the hill, when a cold breeze was blowing. With a world full of sorrow around, he knew, he had not lost anything, though he had not gained anything either. His thoughts were going southwards, when the words of his mother echoed in his ears; they had supported him then and lifted him now. What a coincidence it was--his mother's words resonated in his ears while he sat under the abode of Devi. He was lonely and his seclusion was shared with the solitude of the hill, which was, intermittently, disturbed by the sounds of the temple bells. There were trees around there. Far away a blue curl reminded him of the river they frequented for bathing and immersing idols during the Ganesha festival.

He had planned to go to Bhopal after spending some time at home, but it bored him, for without work it was not possible to survive; boredom pushed him to leave and go to Bhopal, which by train was only three hours journey. The next day he started early so that he could reach on time. After coming out of the railway station, he took a bus to Shahpura. He walked for some distance after getting down from the bus, and reached the house, where he was to stay.

He rang the bell and the owner came out and handed over the keys of his apartment.

Bhopal is located on the edge of Vindhyachal mountain ranges and is popularly comprises seven hills. Bounded by hills, it is a picturesque city surrounded with lakes. The splendid Upper Lake makes Bhopal proud. Tajul Masjid is one of the biggest mosques in the country with imposing domes and minarets; Van-Vihar is a unique national park within the city boundaries, full of wild animals, Museum of Human History, State Museum, Science Centre, and many other places and institutions make it a city of art, culture and wonderful heritage. It reflects the composite culture of India, and has something for everyone. It had something even for Aditya.

He continued his quest to enter the mainstream politics by constantly working with the people. To begin with he started an NGO that worked for the education of the poor kids engaged in garbage collection. To finance his needs, he started practicing at the District Court as a Criminal lawyer. He began representing the needy, the poor and the destitute, who started recognizing him and his work. Soon he was recognized as the one, who cared for the people, especially, those who had no godfather; even the judges started noticing his abilities. Soon he became an indisputable messiah of the poor.

* * *

He began his political career in Bhopal and fought elections for the Councillorship of his local ward,—he lost. Thereafter he led a movement for urban housing for the poor people and his political fortunes fluctuated between despair and ecstasy. Even though, he did not and could not win elections, he was very popular, for the social work he did. However, honesty in political life is recognized very late in life and he had to wait.

A year later, he fought for legislative assembly by polls in the backdrop of his work, but again lost. He wondered why he did not succeed; he could not attribute any reasons for his defeats. He wept in loneliness dejected. His mind and heart were at loggerheads, but the reasons of his failure evaded him. Politics is a complicated affair and baffles the novices.

He set aside many opportunities of a lucrative career and ignored the joys of life to chase his dreams. Most of his friends were already settled in life with good jobs and were financially secure, but he found life going tough for him. What he failed to realize in his zeal for social work was that Politics and doing good to people are two different things, and they solely depended on the fiscal resources, which he did not possess. His brother obtained the degree in Electrical Engineering from IIT Chennai; got a lucrative placement in a Multi National Company and began his life. His father was still working and he could not be of any help to him. It was immensely frustrating.

Amidst the struggle, obstacles and vicissitudes of life, on a chilling dark night, Aditya received a call from Parag, a very practical and shrewd friend. He invited him to his home in Mumbai, to celebrate their reunion after a span of five years, over the weekend. Parag had joined a Multinational Company as Human Resource Development Officer located in Mumbai, and had been living in Mumbai for nearly two years with his wife Riana. Parag told him that he had invited Param and Sam also; both had accepted the invite.

□

Part – 3
SHARED MOMENTS, LEARNING AND ELECTION

20

The stage was set for the meeting, tickets were booked, and packing done. Aditya left Bhopal on Friday evening by Punjab Mail. He was visiting Mumbai for the first time. He boarded the train, and being tired, he tried to sleep instantly. Somebody occupying the adjacent berth was snoring loudly disturbing the sleeping passengers. While he tossed on the narrow berth, he recalled, ruefully, how once he had tried to reach the same city, albeit on some different count, taking a different route and different people, but did not reach the city.

Param started from Chennai, Sam and Diya form Pune and Param kept tracking their journey; it was very typical of him.

Sleep eluded him so he took out the newspaper that he had purchased from the platform. He noticed an article about the rise in the number of cases of sexual abuse against women and children in the country. He thought, "Is the news of rise correct or the truth lies somewhere else. It might be true that such cases are now increasingly reported", and wondered what could be done to check such a social menace.

He recalled, when he was barely ten years old, he had accompanied his parents to attend the marriage of his nephew in a place, Vidisha. It is a well-known place, as it is close to a small but historically important place, Sanchi, renowned for its Stupas. Buddhists from all over the world visit the place to pay respect to the relics of Lord Buddha.

He asked his mother to keep all the best clothes that he would like to wear. He was fond of travelling, the very announcement of attending the function made him excited.

"You have to behave in the function and should remember to give respect to all the elders", his father advised him.

"Yes, I will certainly do.

"Remember there should be no complaints against you".

"He is a good boy, leave him now", interrupted his mother.

They took a train to Vidisha. As soon as they reached there, Aditya touched the feet of his elders and then intermingled with the children of his age and some seniors too, who were more like friends than relatives. In Indian society paying respect to all the elderly relatives by prostration is a norm, without such unconditional surrender respect is not considered given. In India weddings are like festivals, and are celebrated for extended periods.

He played with his friends the whole day and did not come to attend the ceremonies and rituals – for children love to play and enjoy life. Ram was Aditya's favorite relative with whom he shared the childhood games. Ram was his maternal uncle's son, was his coeval and they were natural friends.

Aditya joined one of his uncles, who was going to visit Sanchi the next day, but not before his father warned him not to bother him.

Sanchi is about ten kilometers from Vidisha, and is connected both by rail and road, while travelling on this route; one can see a little hump – the Stupa, at the top of the hill adjoining the road. The splendor of the Stupas cannot be assessed from distance for they yield their imposing beauty from close look. These were constructed somewhere between 2nd and 3rd century BC by Ashoka the Great, though, some additions were made later. Ashoka was governor of Vidisha during his father's rein.

On reaching at the top of the hill one can see three main Stupas. The biggest one is at the top of the hill. These Stupas are characterized by gateways called 'Toranas' on four sides at right angles. They hold relics of Buddha. A close peek at these gates provides insight into the messages carved on these pillars. These sculptures depict the responsibilities of the king from Jataka stories and the life scenes of Buddha. Sanchi records the evolution of beautiful architectural wonders of ancient India.

Not far away from these ancient structures some, ugly modern buildings and shanties that have come up recently, depict the apathy of this generation towards its monuments. Such architectural riches hardly attract a common Indian, who is occupied in his daily struggle for survival and fights the challenges of poverty. Such sight seeing are meant for rich Indians and wealthy foreigners, who can afford to come from distant lands to see them. The taste for art and culture develops only when the belly is full and there is leisure. His parents never cared to visit Sanchi to see the Stupas, though they often went to Vidisha.

They returned back to the venue of the wedding in the evening.

* * *

It was already nightfall and people were taking dinner. After dinner Aditya went to sleep. In such functions, lasting for a week or more, the house turns into a big refugee camp. Tired of the hectic day he slept within no time, with Ram sleeping near him. To his other side was an elder relative of about twenty-one years of age. Late night he found that someone was dragging, his hand for unimaginable gratification. He thought it to be a worst dream and he did not open his eyes to save himself and his relative from embarrassment. That night his relative sleeping close to him tried to play fresh with him.

After one hour of turning and twisting and the struggle to win over the guilt and trauma he could finally sleep. When he woke up in the morning he found that the relative was no more sleeping besides him and there was no trace of him nearby, who later avoided a direct confrontation, till they remained in that house and the wedding was over, as if ashamed of something, which merely confirmed him that it was not a dream but a nightmare. It took a long time before he could come out of that profound guilt that shook his conscience for which he was not responsible.

His sudden relapse into the past made him realize how prevalent and difficult such embracing situation could be. It could be termed as common as it might happen with any child leaving a deep imprint on the mind of the abused child, who suffers such forced indulgences. The level of impact and imprint depends on the kind of perversion one experiences. In Aditya's case it was short of a sexual assault, but it was a forceful one-sided sexual indulgence and an effort on the part of an adult to sexually influence a child. Aditya realized, when it took so long for him to overcome that guilt, then how difficult it would be for a child, who gets sexually assaulted, to forget and come to terms with reality. He never shared this experience with anyone in his family and outside because in Indian society it is taboo to discuss such things in the family or society that wish to remain oblivious to the realities of life under the guise of a false sense of dignity. Children are never encouraged to share such experiences with their parents and therefore, they remain unreported in most of the cases.

He thought of the importance of laws to protect children from abuse and to build awareness among them.

□

21

Aditya reached Mumbai in the morning, took a taxi to go to Parag's house. He had forgotten to ask Parag's address before leaving Bhopal. He rang Parag and got his address. Thank God that Parag was available or else he would be wandering in the city. Later he came to know that Riana, Parag's wife, had wisely recommended him not to switch-off the mobile that night; she was a soft-spoken beautiful lady. Elections had held back Aditya from attending their wedding, a year ago.

He knocked at Parag's door a little after sunlight, though he was the first to disturb his sleep. The door opened and former classmates hugged each other. They had met after a long absence and they felt like talking over the tea, Riana had prepared – past memories came alive. She went to sleep while they talked.

Parag told that since it was not a holiday he was required to go to office. "I have told Param, who has acquiesced, to come directly to the office from airport", he informed.

It was nine o'clock when they left for his office that was like another home for Parag. Param arrived soon; he was the same man unchanged by time. He had a trolley in the right hand and a laptop in the left, was shabbily dressed and wore a T-shirt on a grubby grey trouser, which he alone had the audacity to wear; it betrayed his style. So familiar was his genre that it was not required to actually see him to recognize. He had small deep-set eyes. Even Diya recognized later that he must be Param. Though, from his clothes and idiosyncrasies no one could guess the strength of his character. He bonded the bunch of cronies so nicely that it did not appear that the time had separated them.

Now that he had arrived he would chat with his friends then see his stocks. Despite suffering huge losses in the share market, he continued to trade and give advice to others, about the worth of a stock. Despite suffering losses his friends took his advice, primarily to remain cautious about the stocks he recommended.

Parag was busy with his office work while Param and Aditya sat in the office sipping coffee and chatting.

"How was your trip to Hong Kong?" asked Aditya advancing their tête-à-tête.

"It was amazing. The city is so beautiful that it invites you to stay for a longer duration. Britain had built it, but later China took it over. The city's skyline is dotted with innumerable high-rise buildings. The transport system is fabulous. Besides, it is the financial hub of Asia", replied Param.

"Did you have some work there?"

"No, my uncle went to Hong Kong for three years; he works with the State Bank of India. He was persistently calling for these two years, and I felt that I should go before his deputation ended in another six months. It is an excellent place to visit with family, especially with kids", he said with gaiety.

"How long was your trip?"

"One week, though, I had stayed in Singapore for two days while returning from Hong Kong."

"How is Singapore? What is worth seeing there?"

"It is a city-state. It is so clean and beautiful that one falls in love with it. I stayed in my sister's house. Its remarkable achievements are worth emulating. My sister told me that it was nothing in early fifties of the twentieth century, but now it has miraculously developed and is richer and better than we are on all counts, except one."

"Which one?"

"Population"

"Thank god! We are ahead at least in something." They laughed, enjoying the joke.

"I hear that Singapore has Indian connections!" observed Aditya.

"Yes, the word 'Singapore' is derived from Sanskrit meaning, 'a place of lions'. But, I feel it does not matter for them."

"What all places you visited?"

"I went to Little India, Chinatown and Santosa Island. They have preserved various cultures in a unique way."

"What did you like most about Singapore?"

"I liked their cleanliness, civic amenities, malls, markets and above all their excellent transport system. With a single card one can travel both in a train, bus or a cab. One needs only to swap the card in the automatic machines and no additional assistance is required to pay. Thus, the absence of any conductor with an age-old vending machine in the bus is understandable. What I liked most was the attitude of the people driving a vehicle, who stop and wait in a service lane, till the last pedestrian crosses the road, and then only move on. On major roads, at the crossings, switches are provided, which if pressed, makes the signal red and people can cross the road."

"We should learn from them."

Parag interrupted their discussion when he informed: "I am free now and we can go home and rock the floor." They grinned and left.

* * *

By afternoon, Sam and Diya also joined. Diya was Sam's girlfriend whom he was to marry in three months time. Over lunch, prepared by Riana, they laughed and enjoyed the delicious food. Parag indulged in some pranks for which he was notorious. No one was spared and the atmosphere was lively. They remembered the past confrontations and Parag reminded them about the emotional moments of college days to highlight the trivialities that used to become paramount sometimes.

They discussed elections, debates and the college days and also what other friends were doing. The discussion about spending the evening kept them preoccupied; they remained inconclusive; Sam and Diya went to take a nap while others preferred to roam around.

Parag had promised Aditya to show the grand house of his favourite movie star, which was in the vicinity, but was guarded like a fortress. Celebrities in India get protection from police, but common man is left to fend for himself. The law and order situation is so precarious that a lady could be raped somewhere in the absence of a better law enforcement machinery, yet police is forced to perform VIP duties, providing security to the rich and the powerful than securing the life of a common man. Police is available for searching the stolen buffalos of influential people, but, it is not there to check crime; dacoities are committed, rapes take place, traffic woes multiply, innocent citizens are beaten up with impunity, corruption abounds and the law enforcing agencies look the other way.

Dirty beaches characterize the beautiful Arabian Sea. People living near the sea-line pitch their jhuggies; slums mushroom and there is nothing, but human beings, dirtying all over the place. Wherever one ganders, only people are seen at every visible place, people occupied with work and running in hurry. Nobody knows from where they come. Expensive bungalows, the abode of the rich and the famous dot the sea-beaches. Dirty beaches are the places for the poor to defecate. Busy roads to approach them characterized Juhu beach in Mumbai.

They reached the beach; the water was black. Mumbai's waste disposal in the sea has made even the sea look dirty. That happens when more than 15 million people live in a city and to half of them there is no clean drinking water and waste disposal facilities. More than half of India's population is poor and for non-availability of latrines defecates in the open, making it one of the biggest open latrines in the world. Who cares for the poor; can they take care of themselves? They too get their share of free bees of a welfare state that compels them to live a disgusting life.

They sat there for half an hour, drank coconut water, ate pani puri with tamarind water and left after the day's enjoyment. Before they left, they contributed their share to the garbage, as the shopkeeper dumped the garbage in a small sewer leading to the Arabian Sea. Mumbai, despite all that can be said against it, is a beautiful place and they loved the city. It pained them to see its environment being degraded even by the educated people. It is the common fate of all the good cities in India, proving the theory of the tragedy of commons.

By the time they returned, they had shopped, roamed, ate and enjoyed in all possible ways. Aditya was almost a broke and told Param, sadly, "I have not earned much in my life and there is no question of savings. I do not know what will happen to me?"

"You may have not earned money, but you have learned much more precious things than money – the goodwill of your constituency", said a sanguine Param after sensing the difficulties of Aditya, and both of them smiled.

"Even though we earned, we lost everything, thanks to Param's advice. It would have been better not to earn. Anybody can surmise that it is better not to earn than to lose all one has earned on a foolish advice", said Parag to lift the mood further and tease Param, who had advised him to buy shares of a company that vanished from the market after inflicting heavy losses on the shareholders.

"Mall is a perfect place to regale and lighten our purses", said Riya to break the emotional tension. They took a quick look of a nearby mall ate snacks after they were tired of window-shopping. Then came the moment, for which everybody was desperately waiting – the booze time with lot of intoxicated chatting.

* * *

The long awaited bottles were opened so were the packets of snacks. Riana looked puzzled and nervous, for she was not sure how would she handle these friends, once they are drunk. Aditya chose not to drink as usual. It comforted her that somebody would be there to keep a check and she could have some sleep.

The mat and bedding were spread over the floor on which papers were placed to keep snacks and some yellow and white bottles. Biryani was the perfect dish after everyone had gulped down large measures of liquor. It was cheers all along with lots of drunken reveling. Riana held back to Pepsi and said: "Oh! They are reviving the good old days", commented Riana.

Aditya and Parag were teasing Param, and reminded him about the comments, "Chotu, choti aankh vale chor (you thief with small eyes)", by Jagat Sir, who was head of the sports department in the college and had once teased Param for his dismal show in a volleyball match they lost. They laughed with adrenalized voices, while ladies were amused.

Someone commented, "when Param was born he was bald, even now he is bald, and it seems he would continue to be bald, perpetually and who knows his kids too will be bald", at which more laughter ensued.

"Ah! The past memories of the college days will ever haunt us. An oasis in the desert of life", commented Parag.

"Do you remember when Sam proposed a girl from the commerce class?" Aditya tried to remind them.

"Yes, but before he could propose, she called him brother", said Param while others laughed and Dia blushed.

"Aditya, you – 'Dewas vale' from village; whatever he did was reminiscent of his village. Oye Param! You small eyed alien, keep mum", warned Sam.

"Do you guys remember when Param was after Maya and luring her", said Aditya.

"Yes, the very next day our teacher had caught them red handed, kissing in the class, when everybody was gone after the last lecture. He threatened to kick them out of the college, had it not been for Maya's influential father, who doused the fire", said Sam while others laughed, hysterically.

"But, you should appreciate my talent that the very next day she was with me", replied Param to regain his self-respect.

"However, Param never told us, what happened when Maya had come to study in his room, a night before the exams", asked Parag. Riana, expressing sympathy for Param, asked Parag to spare him.

"Yes, I know both flunked," replied Sam and more laughter followed.

"Where is she now?" asked Aditya.

"She is with a leading News channel looking after marketing", replied Param.

"Are you in touch with her?"

"Yes, she has invited me to attend her marriage in Bangalore."

"Will you go?"

"Why not", another burst of laughter.

Some more comments about Raj, Sunny and few others followed. Sam was lost somewhere while Diya talked, enthusiastically, about her friends and college. Sam stopped drinking after his fiancé started. Riana intruded their exchanges and tried to comfort the one picked by Parag, who pulled and poked, pricked and peeled off smile from his jokes.

"How is Puja?" somebody asked. Aditya pretended to be sleeping. Nobody asked further as they knew that he was neither aware where Puja was, nor was interested in her discussion.

By the small hours of morning, everyone was fast asleep. It was difficult to tell who slept first. May be all slept at once? Who knows? Perhaps Riana!

□

22

The next morning the sun rose with all its glory, the small appearing long night was over and the drowsy company recovered their senses and packed them with a new energy. Parag left for the office as he had urgent work in his office. Others left for Silver Beach where they took photographs. Diya and Sam left for his maternal aunt's home and thereafter proceeded to Pune. After a long session of chatting and roaming over sandy beaches they left; there was chill in the air following the extravagant euphoria.

Param and Aditya left for Borivali. They took a taxi to reach the local suburban railway station, Andheri. On the way, they saw skyscrapers dotting the entire route. They are the symbols of increasing islands of prosperity amid the ocean of poverty, as India is growing so is its poor. At the station they parted. Aditya took a local train to the east to meet his niece in Borivali. Param proceeded to the west to meet Sunny. They took ride in the Mumbai suburban train, which is the lifeline of this city. After every four to five minutes, there is a local train – a frequency that makes it possible for this city to move. People travelling in the train boast that the city would not have grown so vastly were local trains not there. In fact, the first Indian passenger train chucked there.

He reached Borivali, met his niece and left to join Param and Sunny. He took another local train to come back to catch up with them. On his return journey, looking out from the window of the running train gave him strange feelings.

Mumbai is a great city in many ways. It has all the riches and it has all the poverty; it is clean and beautiful yet there are filthy places; it has beautiful skyscrapers and large slums; it has lot of money both black and white and is connected to the underworld; it is humane, yet hardhearted; it is inclusive and at the same time it is exclusive. It is a maximum city, a paradox that baffles. He thought, "I hated the city from a distance, but on closer view I love it." The strange magic of this city keeps everyone spell bound. It has something for everyone to live for and survive, for it has a challenging environment.

They had tried a lot, but had failed to convince Sunny to join them to share good times, the previous day. Sunny had been their favorite pastime. Whenever they were devoid of any enjoyment in the hostel, they banked on Sunny, and when any one was in need of support, Sunny was always there like a good angel. He gave emotional support to everyone; leave alone the books, which were torn off to distribute amongst them to read a night before the exam. He was a constant source of entertainment when other revelries were not available. He was a fertile ground to plant all naughty ideas his friends might have had. The memory of that day still endures when under the guise of a serious discussion they had implanted a bomb in his room under his cot. When it exploded he was sure that it must have been his naughty friends' brainchild. Though after the incident, he was not annoyed, and they were not apologetic.

Sunny had not changed much, slim body with a visible tummy and a receding hairline. Who would lose all the hair first, Sunny or Param, was a debatable issue among them.

Now they could make out the reason why Sunny did not join them yesterday. A family was visiting them with a marriage proposal. Like Param, Sunny was also trying, frantically, to get married, but he was not lucky to find a suitable match yet. They asked about his job, his struggle after he lost his father and about his visit to European countries the previous month to establish an office for his company.

"How is your preparation for polls going on, Aditya?" he asked.

"Fine is the only thing I have to say at the moment, though I have lost all the elections I have contested."

"I believe you will win this time."

"Hope so."

There was some silence when Aditya asked again. "What about your marriage?"

"We are in the process of short listing two proposals and would take a final call in a week's time. Promise that you will attend the marriage."

"I will certainly come."

They talked for some more time about the shared experiences of college days and about other friends, till the time came for them to part. They left after his mother blessed them.

On their way back, Param told him about the flat he had booked. Aditya however, told him, "I have started accepting cases in the district court to survive and buying a property is a far-fetched dream." He looked at the setting sun to hide his eyes from Param that were welled up with tears. He had some important work the next day so he stayed on yet another day.

□

23

Aditya called Guru in the evening and they decided to meet the following day at Colaba near Gateway of India from where they would travel to Elephanta Island. To meet him was another important reason of his visit to Mumbai. Aditya had introduced Parag to him when he came to Delhi when they were in the college. Parag had met Guru a couple of times after coming to Mumbai and was in touch with him.

Guru was Aditya's school senior living in Mumbai, who belonged to a very humble background and always wanted to be a fighter pilot. He toiled to clear all the exams, and finally became a fighter pilot in the Indian Air Force. He was widely respected both in his school and the town. He was a role model for others, who had proved that it is not only possible to live one's dream, but go beyond it and catch a falling star. However, he left IAF later to become a Professor in TISS, Mumbai. Why he left his dream job is not known to anybody. It seems that he was not satisfied for there was no war to satisfy his dreams or action. May be, he left the job so that he could exclusively devote to his commitment to serve his country.

Aditya reached early at the Gateway of India and waited for Guru to arrive. While he waited, he got a chance to see the Gateway of India from close quarters. He observed that something was written on the top of the splendid arch, reading which, he learned that it was erected to mark the arrival of King George V and Queen Mary in the year 1911.

He also saw Hotel Taj Mahal Palace. Many people were taking photographs in front of the hotel. It is a magnificent building where the rich and mighty come and stay at seaside. Knowing that he had to wait for some more time before Guru arrived, he thought of taking a drink and relaxing at Leopold Café. He had barely finished when somebody greeted him from behind.

"It is great to see you back Aditya. Hope everything is fine. I was so excited to see you. You had surprised me greatly, when you gave me a call yesterday night that you are in Mumbai", said Guru.

"I thought of meeting you the moment I got your number from Parag. But Mumbai is so big that it requires a lot of time to travel from one place to another. Besides, I had to see your convenience."

"How is Parag? Why did he not come?"

"He had to leave for his office as always he had some urgent work to attend".

"How is everybody at home?"

"Everybody is fine. Thank you. What about you?"

"Great, I am good. Did you see the Elephanta Island?"

"No."

They decided to go to the Elephanta Island, and took a ferry from Colaba, near the Gateway of India. They sat on top of the ferry from where they could see the skyline of Mumbai at one side and ships sailing at the horizon and a distant faint looking Island on the other.

"How is your preparation going for the Assembly Elections?" asked Guru.

"Sir, I had lost all the previous elections I fought", Aditya replied with a deep sigh.

"I feel I will not be able to win elections and may even not succeed in that tricky world."

"Don't give up so easily, for history is replete with examples of people, who were never disheartened and, eventually, won their battle. It is a known fact that those who never gave up succeeded. There are some fundamental truths and similarities, which are common among successful people despite remarkable differences in their behavioral pattern. These fundamental truths can make anybody and everybody successful in their own ventures. There may be disagreements about the relative importance of these different attitudes and habits or dimensions of personality, nevertheless, there cannot be any denying the fact they establish that a man is capable of achieving the impossible, if he does not lose heart."

"I have started feeling that I am a normal human being good for nothing."

"I have always told people how a normal individual with even an average IQ can achieve phenomenal success in his career. I have discovered these fundamentals while pursuing my ambition of becoming an IAF Officer and later."

"How is that possible when a person gets defeated every time?"

"You should not get disheartened."

"Is it possible?"

"One should work on improving personal skills if one wants to achieve higher and difficult goals in one's life. The first step is to set the goal, the first thing for everyone to be successful. Without a goal we may end up as nobody. A goalless life is a great source of frustration, which people scarcely realize." He paused for a brief while, looked away from Aditya, who asked, "When did you think of becoming a pilot?"

"I conceptualized the goal long back in my school days. I know many of my friends, who never thought what they wanted to achieve in their life and they ended up either nowhere or somewhere they never intended to, and now they are discontented with their lives." He took a sip from his glass of coca cola and spoke again, as if possessed."

"I too have a goal, but it eludes me."

"The decision about a goal assists in directing all of our focus and attention with the limited or unlimited energy in achieving the goal. We all know that a concentrated beam of sun after passing through a lens can burn anything, whereas a simple beam without the desired medium cannot. Learning from it, why we should ourselves not direct our energy in one particular direction – the direction of our goal."

"I want to become a successful politician. It requires that I should be elected to some office. I tried for Councilor I lost, tried for MLA and I lost. I cannot survive like that."

"You might have set your goal but setting goal alone is not sufficient. One should find the wherewithal to achieve the goal as the next step. This requires finding ways and means to achieve it. We have many resources available today, I often suggest to my students to get information regarding various career options. I also advice them to meet people who work in the concerned field, talk to seniors in school and college, and consult relatives and make appropriate and extensive use of internet. As a result, you would be amazed to know, most of my students come back and tell it has helped them a great deal. In politics too, one should have a mentor to guide."

Aditya did not say anything, but continued to listen. The ferry continued the journey towards the island, screaming many times to warn other ferries passing through the same lane, either returning or going in different directions.

"There is a word of caution: our goals should be as realistic as possible, as we can not think of becoming somebody, if we don't have the required talent and inclination. The word realistic means that there should be sufficient time and resources required to achieve or decide upon a goal. If one wants to become a billionaire in a day, it would be considered insanity in any normal circumstance, but if it were through lottery or a lucky draw or a bank robbery, it is a different story", said Guru and continued, "as a next step one should put in hard work to achieve the goal. This being, one of the most important steps, requires action on the part of the person. People think of success in many complex ways, but I explain it in a very simple way. Success is a multiplicative function of hard work and intelligence."

He wrote on a piece of tissue paper, lying on the table, meant to clean hands, 'success = hard work * intelligence' and explained, "success can also be explained as a multiplicative function of attitude and aptitude." He wrote again, 'success = attitude * aptitude' and handed it over to Aditya, who kept it inside his pocket after looking at it several times.

"Hard work is nothing but an attitude or could also be termed as an outcome of an attitude – the attitude to excel. Aptitude is one's ability and capability to perform something that could be measured in terms of intelligence. Normal people can also succeed by increasing the quantum of hard work, for the product of hard work and intelligence would still remain same as required to succeed. This provides a ray of hope for everybody on earth, especially to those, who may not be exceptionally intelligent, but have exceptional capability to toil. With perseverance one can compensate for aptitude or intelligence. That is the reason many average people have achieved great successes on earth like Edison, Newton and many more."

"Thus, the silver line is – if one is weak or lacks success despite efforts, then one ought to work twice as hard as others whom one wants to compete", concluded Aditya.

"Yes, but, I feel one should not be swept away by blind competition. One should have his unique identity and goals, which could also be achieved without being in competition with anyone. Our efforts should not be to amuse others, but to delight ourselves. We can perform by setting our own standards, nay chasing others heedlessly", assured Guru to an agitated Aditya with his eyes fixed on the horizon.

They reached the Island where the ferry anchored: they were instructed to return back before 5:00 pm when the last ferry leaves back for Mumbai. It was a beautiful place, surrounded by water from all the sides, the water touching the mangroves and waves splashing it many times before high tide sank them completely. The thick mangroves resisted the encroachment of the sea.

There was a small train waiting for the passengers to shuttle them to the place from where the steps towards Elephanta temple would start. Archeologically, it is a significant place near Mumbai. The steps were large, but appeared small due to shops occupying space on both the sides. The shops were selling variety of items including idols, toys, chocolate, pickle, mango, corn and other things of tourist interest. There were many monkeys on the island that made children happy, but proved a nuisance to the shop owners and women.

After visiting the surrounding structures, they reached at the top of the hill near the main temple. These rock cut sculptures were carved out in 5th-6th century AD. There are seven caves: the main temple is located in the biggest cave. It has giant three-headed rock cut Mahadev or Shiva sculpture called "Sadashiva", which has three heads representing three significant aspects. First one represents, The Creator; second, The Preserver; and third, The Destroyer. At other side was a giant Shivling; people were taking its photographs; some tourists were looking at it curiously. Some others were performing religious rites at it. Aditya seemed uninterested in structures, but was interested in Guru's company. After seeing the site extensively and taking a stroll around the island they sat on a platform. The site was perfect as they were able to see the skyline of Mumbai at a farther distance at one side and the port-JNPT at the other.

"We can see and assess the height of buildings from a distant place or what is going on at different places. Similarly we should evaluate our Performance."

"How? Can you explain that?"

"If one wants to be successful, then one needs to be objective in his approach. One should be honest, objective and critical so that one does not deceive oneself while assessing one's performance, like we review performance of others, dispassionately. Performance should be regularly evaluated, to gauge the progress, considering both its strengths and weaknesses. This helps in setting the benchmarks to improve performance and always chimes with the demand of the time."

"I will try to organize my life as you say, but this doesn't seem new to me. I accept that I was never organized in my efforts. Besides, I have failed to analyze my defeats, rationally."

"You not only need to be organized, but you should always make efforts to improve. Improvements should be made on the basis of performance evaluation. Corrective steps should be taken to make it competitive after evaluating the performance. It's like the game tennis in which a player, after losing one set to the opponent, reflects and analyzes the reasons responsible for the loss of a set. This helps in changing the strategy or adopting other measures to improve chances of winning.

Similar is the power of belief. If a person has faith in his abilities and believes in himself, he would achieve any goal that he sets before him. It is one of the greatest qualities that successful people possess. I enquired many people about the secret of their success, and their reply was, 'have faith in your abilities'. Failure may sometimes baffle, but if we persist in our efforts, and have faith in ourselves, then nothing can defeat us. At the end success is ours."

"You speak like a success Guru, but I like the formula for success."

Aditya was looking at JNPT, which was visible from there. It was difficult to imagine how the time had elapsed when the watch showed half past four and Guru reminded him, "It is time to move or we would be stranded on this Island for the night." They hurriedly walked towards the ferry.

* * *

The water had risen up to the leaves of mangroves indicating high tide. The sun was about to set. He was still looking at the passing ships and their destinations. Some ships were anchored near the port waiting for their turn. Far away at the horizon he could see some ships, and their journey symbolized the ship of life in search of the destination.

The ferry was full of people. It sounded the alarm indicating that it was ready to leave. They rushed back and took their seats. It moved after de-anchoring and they decided to sit downstairs, to have cold drinks and snacks.

While Aditya still looked outside at horizon, Guru continued, "Burn yourself in the fire of struggle, and you will see the glitter of gold on your face that the world will not fail to recognize. Endurance is such a great quality that it fills you with tolerance and love for others. Serenity allows frustration to dissipate and recoup. It helps in understanding the circumstances and people around you better. It also makes the interpersonal relation better and enhances respect for one another, which is most important for a politician." The mention of politician made his eyes shine with an effulgence of his face.

"What else do you think is required for being a successful politician?" He asked.

"I am not a politician so I cannot tell you about that profession, but I can tell you what universal qualities a politician should possess. Be optimistic in relation to others; do not look people from the prism of experience alone, but through the light of wisdom and love."

"I have lost my love too, I loved Puja, though today, I know not where she is?"

"Always remember that there is no greater sin than brooding about the sin itself. Those who brood about and think negatively, those who don't move on and remain struck by the disaster even after it has left, loose the chance nature provides to be happy and contented. There is no room for despair, even if we are struck by unexpected disasters in life, we should move on and try to look happy and mingle with people to find hope.

If something is done with dedication and devotion, then even the universal power helps to achieve it – 'God helps them who help themselves.' You will find these magical words written in many great books. You will hear these traits from many saints and noble souls. You should sow the seeds of thought. When you act with all devotion you will see the transformation of that thought into reality and action. Our thoughts are the driving force of our action."

"How can I change my thoughts?"

"One should always talk to oneself. There should always be a thought running in the sub-conscious mind that 'I want to achieve my target' or 'I want to be so and so'. There is, however, a difference between positive self-talk and obsession with a thought; you have to prevent yourself from such obsessions."

"Does talking to oneself really help?"

"Yes. Besides, resoluteness of a person determines how the person treads the path of difficulty. With single mindedness one can achieve greater heights even when facing adversity. There is a subtle difference between success and failure and among people on either side of success and failure. Though people differ very little in their abilities, yet, purposefulness developed and possessed by them brings a lot of difference in the level of their achievement."

"You remind me of the words of a great poet, Iqbal, 'khudi ko kar buland itna ki har taqdeer se pahele khuda bande se khud puchee bata teri raza kya hai.' "

"Yes, I have seen it working it in many cases including my own when I had to appear for Pilot Aptitude Test, which people consider to be the toughest in the selection process of the Air Force. This statement, if kept in the mind, coupled with hard work can achieve miracles. Those who use it see miracles actually happening in their lives."

"Would you like to take something else sir?" asked the attendant in the ferry while Guru thanked him and continued to speak.

"Being an extrovert assists in winning friends and becoming part of a group very easily. It assists in coping with potential problems. One has to be tolerant while dealing with people. Sometimes the individual or the group with whom we interact tests our patience sub-consciously. In such a scenario, we should be careful not to react to the comment or undesirable behavior of playful friends. Love shown to others combined with tolerance removes the feeling of rage or hate. When we remain unaffected by the undesirable behavior of the person, the person inflicting the blow undergoes a sea change in attitude."

"These qualities seem more important to be a politician."

"They are essential for anything one does. Though there are other things as well: be gracious to the people you interact with; help people and they would love you. One should be assertive enough to avoid getting used and avoid the sense of guilt arising out of it. You should develop some hobbies and habits, as they assist in improving the personality. They are good bet to fall back when we feel dejected and disheartened; they build self-confidence and enhance self-esteem."

"Yes, I remember my mother telling me to read good books, as they are the source of tremendous energy, which could be employed to achieve the goal by sustaining the momentum of action for long, with zeal and zest."

"Always mingle and socialize with people who are constructive in their approach and do not dampen your spirit by cautious advice. Some people spread cynicism, we must either guide them to escape from it or get away or remain aloof from them", Guru finished while Aditya was keenly watching him.

His loneliness and failures had made him forget the teachings he had received from his mother. But this gentle reminder from Guru rejuvenated him. Charged with Guru's ideas he shared his thoughts with him.

"It is so coincidental that few years ago, my mother told me things that helped me in facing the challenges I faced then. When I was on the verge of losing everything including my studies, she provided me extraordinary courage", said Aditya.

"Should I finish or do you want more?"

"Aye."

"Now I will tell you one of the biggest secrets of my life. It seems very unusual, but it is true that I have always listened to my inner voice or the messages of the universal cosmic power. These messages I call inner voice. I have always realized that whenever I was in any doubt or difficulty some invisible power has guided me and I have heard the inner voice. It is my strong belief that everybody gets some divine message that guides him, though it takes time and faith to reach a stage when one can listen to and comprehend these messages, which we understand as the inner voice."

"But, people have different opinions about it, and question such thing."

"Most of us either doubt it or just want not to hear it or are incapable of hearing it. Some build a strong defensive mechanism that inhibits the voice reach their minds, or some remain so occupied in worldly affairs that they can't hear it. I believe in spirituality and mysticism, which are a special gift to us and is a guiding force for the humanity to grow towards future and perfection. It is this inner voice that has led me to achieve the unachievable, which seemed impossible by my own standards and that of others for me."

"Are you trying to convey that we should become mystic and leave rationality?"

"No. I never say that. What I say is combine rationality, objectivity and spiritualism. Spiritualism is not irrational like blind faith and black magic."

"Does spiritualism mean listening to the inner voice?"

"No. We all are part of the cosmic world and not different from it. It is like the relation between the leaves and the roots of a tree. Can they be different?"

"No"

"Then how can we be different from our creator?"

"I do not understand."

"There is a universal power, a giant wheel that controls everything. We are part of it as we are part of this universe. Thus, we can always listen to it like leaves listen to the roots."

"Something guides us when we close our eyes. It happened with me. The one who hears the inner voice never faces miseries even in the face of difficulties and other discomfitures. I have stopped hearing my inner voice for some time and that is the reason why I am miserable. I believe in your words. Faith and belief in ourselves enable us to hear the inner voice."

"It is our inner voice and our potential that prompt us many times to predict things, though, I would sound a word of caution here: if one uses the inner voice for personal gains and gives the impression that one can foretell future then one is destined to doom, and the power to hear inner voice vanishes. It should be used for noble causes and sparingly used for greater public good."

"Have you ever used it?"

"It may sound strange, but is true, while watching the world cup football, 2014, I combined the pattern of different teams and statistics, and predicted the winning teams before every match correctly, and eventually correctly predicted the winner of the world cup. Only once my prediction was wrong when I trusted my expectations, ignoring the inner voice. Another time I used it to gain in stocks, but soon I stopped after realizing that I was getting sucked up in the trap of greed; I sold all the shares and gave away the profits."

"I am amazed to know that. But, what about objectivity?"

"Our expectations, objective view of the world and inner voice should always be kept independent of each other, and then the combination of all of them can help us in assessing the outcome. The successful people do it. If it is used for greed than it vanishes."

"Why do we fail if inner voice tells us everything?" asked Aditya seeking an explanation.

"Failure is a result of our efforts not of the inner voice. Inner voice is not a magic that can make you succeed without efforts. Thus, it is wrong to assume that if one hears the inner voice one can be successful. Even those who fail can hear the inner voice and those who hear the inner voice too can fail. It tells, what is required to be done, and what one may do for betterment. Inner voice is a guiding force, which points the right direction. It may tell that one should be a fighter pilot or an artist. If we do not put the required efforts towards establishing a goal then we may not succeed. Success is purely an outcome of our efforts in the desired direction."

"Why do we fail then?" asked Aditya. The burden of his failures was evident in his deliberations.

Guru tried to reassure him and said, "There are failures even when there are efforts. One should have the ability to absorb the adverse impact of failures and one should learn to accept them – to overcome them, learn from them and then move on to become successful in the long run. Those who keep worrying about the failures and do nothing suffer. Whenever failures come, they come to test our capabilities."

"Does that mean it has limitations?"

"No. It is a force that remains with human being because we are a part of the universal energy. To understand the inner voice one has to understand the universe and one has to view the universe as a whole. If a drop of water is taken out of the ocean than the ocean becomes ocean minus a drop; the drop seems so insignificant that we do not consider it, but nobody including scientists can claim that when a drop is removed from the ocean, it is the same ocean. Taking this analogy to universe, the ocean can be thought of as universe and man a drop."

"But the universe is so big how can we get message from it?"

"As a part of the universe, if we desire to hear the inner voice or the messages of the universe to get the directions and indications in life, we can. Nevertheless, all the successful people do not hear it, as it is not a precondition for success. On many occasions we say that, 'I am going to make it or not', it is because we get the clue from somewhere about our success or failure, after the action is already done; it is nothing but the inner voice. The secrets of success are evident at many places, one only needs to find them, to learn from them and implement them in our lives."

"Can everyone hear it?"

"The people who do not wish to hear it could never hear the inner voice; even those who wish to hear it can't hear it every time, as it requires immense concentration and mediation to understand it, which is not possible for everyone. This is the connection between spiritualism and the inner voice. Inner voice is useful when one tries to achieve something that seems beyond reach and is unachievable. It assists those, who feel themselves to be a part of the universal soul. The Upanishads teach us that we all are the part of the universal soul."

"People say we control our destiny."

"Yes, in a way, provided we know what we want. The universal power helps us in achieving our desired goals. We may feel that we are in control of a situation, but it is the invisible power that does it. It does not mean that the outcomes of the world are predetermined, but the outcomes are a result of the desires of human beings and the efforts to achieve them, provided one puts in his finest efforts. When we put our best efforts invisible power puts vigour in our soul to excel. It is the mix of these that people perceive as one's capabilities leading to success. If it were individual capabilities alone one would never fail. People fail because it is more than the capabilities that determine success."

"May be your words would help me in achieving my aim in life. I was on the verge of giving up before meeting you, but I am sure now I will achieve my goal and dream of my life. You have reminded me of my mother's teachings, she once told me to never give up."

The sun was about to set behind the Arabian Sea and it was time for Aditya to leave. The ferry was nearing the Gateway of India.

"Aditya, in this world everything is possible. It is a magical world, what one thinks can happen. No effort goes in vain provided the spirit and efforts do not desert. But this applies only to those thoughts that acquire the wheels of action and pace of zeal. When wings are given to one's imaginations then significant spectacles of arts are created. You ask any successful man and he would tell you that his life is full of magical experiences; many a time they confess that they never imagined the kind of grand success they achieved."

"Whatever you tell me is nothing less than a magical experience for me, I feel like dreaming", said Aditya, hearing which Guru could not resist sharing his concealed thoughts and experiences.

"I will share with you the dialogue I had, with the universal power once, which I have never shared with anyone so far. Once I failed in my life to clear the exam for IAF despite putting my best efforts, I was dejected and my spirits were sagging, but there was something that drove me to continue my struggle. I told the universal power that, 'I would continue to work hard in achieving my goal even if my failures stalk my life. I accept defeat, but am not ready to quit, I concede defeat and admit that I had put less effort or I do not deserve success with current level of efforts. However, I refuse to accept defeat from trying. I would die trying rather than acquiesce defeat of my initiative and my soul.' One should have tenacity and perseverance for the goal and there should be a dialogue with the universal power that, 'I have given my best, now it is your turn'." Guru concluded.

Guru hugged him, and bid him adieu. Aditya took a bus, waved back at him as if thanking him for all the encouragement he gave; Guru watched him go and thoughts came huddling that he too had faced a similar situation, when he had left the job he loved, to achieve higher aims.

* * *

He took a bus and travelled from Colaba to Andheri. While he sat comfortably, he felt a gush of a strange energy in his body. He could not understand the energy and the source it might have originated from, but when he closed his eyes he felt a gentle caress. It indicated him that he had to struggle that would produce success for him. Being perplexed, he opened his eyes again and again, and thought that his imagination and desires are producing that kind of hallucinations for him. He felt so light, as if he was flying in the air or suspended in the space as he entered in meditation. The freshness of the life touched his mind and soul, but he could not comprehend the divine experience. His mother's words, spoken long ago, and what Guru spoke not long ago, echoed in his mind giving him the strength to start a new life.

Aditya picked his luggage and left for the railway station. Param left next morning. The venue was deserted in the morning. The host had left for office, but the marry talking and the bonhomie of the previous nights was visible all over; beddings, empty bottles and the disorderly room and the silent TV. However, the echoes of their shared moments were audible. Friendship is such a beautiful thing; Aditya wished Parag continued to prove him wrong. The friends had parted company.

□

24

He was full of energy and zeal after his return from Mumbai, for travel and meeting friends rekindled his spirit. Once again he was ready to dedicate all his efforts towards his goal. The elections were not far. He met with various electorates and stakeholders to get connected with them, organically. He expanded work of his NGO and touched the people hitherto untouched with his work. Six months were over after his return. The polls for the Legislative assembly of the state were announced.

It was a new dawn, a reddish orange and saffron sun is emerging from the horizon over the top of the trees that looked greenish grey with black shadows, the invisible hand painting the blue sky with whitish red brush, filling the space with golden colour, splashing the colours of freshness on which birds were flying, spreading the hope that a new destiny is awaiting him. He looked, at the sky concentrating at infinity, out of the window of his house, and beseeched to cosmic power for his success. It was the day to fill the nomination for contesting the polls.

He prepared himself and left home to fill the papers for election to the member of legislative assembly. He entered in the room of the election officer without noticing the old rusted nameplate, with a name engraved in black and white, hanging before the door of the office. Destiny had once chosen to keep them apart, now he could not believe his eyes, the college life came before his eyes in quick succession and passed through in a single moment. The officer sitting in front of him was a lady, who looked at him with surprise first, and sympathy later, which he did not like and care for.

She was Puja, who became a senior Government Officer and was posted as election officer here, barely a month ago, for smooth conduct of the elections. He never expected that he would confront her and discover her success like this. The life had promised so much when it brought two lost hearts together. Today they were together yet separated by deep chasm of insulated love. A life in search of the reasons for existence struggled hard to establish its identity.

"Please sign here", said the familiar voice. He obliged. Both wanted to ask beyond it, but were prevented by time and place. He controlled his emotions, filled the form with his supporters and left the office without looking back.

Puja never imagined that life would come back full circle to her after they left each other in the college without a word for future. She had joined JNU for her masters, and continued her studies to become a top government servant. When she was in Delhi she used to hear about Aditya from the friends and cheap local newspapers. She had tried once, but could not meet him. One day she noticed his disappearance from the newspapers. Preoccupied in her studies, she almost forgot him. Later she had learned about him, whatever little she could, from Parag, but he never updated her that Aditya had shifted to Bhopal.

While Aditya plunged in the ocean of his dreams and struggle, she continued her studies for her goal. She appeared once and failed in interview. She tried again and was successful. She joined the service and left for training. That was the last time she talked to her college friend Parag, who despite knowing everything, kept it a secret and never divulged it to Aditya thinking that it would add injury to his failure. But destiny has other plans to reveal the truths.

"When will you marry?" asked his father once, at which she had replied, "I know not", in a sullen voice. She could never comprehend if it was the regret of leaving him that forced her to remain single. More than contrition, it was that she did not learn to compromise. She recalled, how vociferously, her father had opposed her friendship with him, when she had broken the news of her relation to him after coming back from the trek, when he had enjoined, "No. Not in any case will I allow that to happen."

While he strove hard to hide his emotions from others he could not deceive his own heart. He thought, "Why are you lost in the silence of memories, as if your image is forgotten in the darkness of the night, as if your voice is lost in the clamor of the noise, as if a dream is lost in the memory, as if you have become anonymous waiting for a dream, as if the river is left with only a bank without the splash of water or the gush of its flow, as if the smoke left the ash alone to struggle and bear the pain of life, why have you become a stranger.

Drowned in the depths of the past from where the mind would not try to venture out, today heart implores for time, to come to a halt. Like the bygone ages that have been bounded in a moment, all the memories of the life are stuck in that moment. There were dreams in the closed eyes, but now only memories lie in my open eyes. Every moment was a prize that we got, when we lived happily, regardless of the memories that permeate into sadness. Your name comes on my lips, but leaves moistened eyes. The one, I strive to find, who could comprehend my thoughts, but only echoes of loneliness live in those exertions."

That jungle, those mountains, the sleepy, dry sparsely filled river were the things frequented by him during autumns of his fast changing, still slow progressing life. After the passage of so many years, his eagerness to cement a lasting relation was rekindled. Her mere thought made him swim in the ocean of hope after coming out of the valley of despair. The last encounter did not belie his expectations rather it rejuvenated his spirit and inspired to tread a path of immense satisfaction. He was too optimistic since he forgot that the world changes and so does the relation. He had to travel ahead with time and going back was neither easy nor a desirable option.

* * *

Aditya became engrossed in his busy life once again, forgetting last week's incidence. It was difficult for him to get married without any work, though he did not marry for a different reason. He himself was not sure whether it was his love for Puja, or the burden of failing to express that he wanted her when he had the opportunity. However, he too like Puja neither desired to force himself nor he longed both of them to compromise with their dreams. "No sane parents could have allowed their daughter to marry a wanderer, who had no secure future", he thought.

* * *

One day he was campaigning for votes and support when he saw a bête noire standing in front of him staring at him. It seemed a familiar face to him. For a moment it inspired fear in him. He was Kallu, the person who had treated him so dreadfully, when he had tumbled to his village accidently, with his friends.

Kallu and Rajesh had abandoned the village two years back once they lost the business due to the construction of a new bypass and the urban sprawl, which had taken a toll on the local business. They had started working in a private company in Bhopal. For last one-year, they were working for his NGO without his knowledge. They had heard about him, as he was very popular among the poor and impoverished people, through his work in the locality, and had decided to work for him. They believed in him so much that they boasted, "He alone could solve the problems of the people." They left no effort in ensuring that his good work reached to the people and they supported him in the election. However, they did not know that he is the one, who had fled his home, and to whom they had treated so shabbily.

Aditya did not avoid the encounter and asked squarely, "Do you remember me?" He overcame his fear to pose this question. Humility is a great quality that he had in plenty. He thought how stupid and immature he was to leave home to pursue his dreams.

They could have been caught if not then, then a little later. Man follows a pattern while doing anything. No activity of a human being could be termed as absolutely random, and it cannot be glossed over if investigated diligently. Certain behaviors remain incomprehensive or crimes remain mystery because we do not possess the determination to unearth them. "How easy it could have been for our kith and kin to diagnose that we were up to something unnatural when we were meeting regularly at a distant and lonely place not allowing any other person to be in our group", he thought.

The deviations from statistical averages always have a message to tell. Like in their case they used to either play at home or sleep or watch TV at home during their summer vacations, but they were doing something else. They were meeting only limited friends, going to selected places at particular time and deviating from their long-term habits. Human beings, being so organized, renders people prisoner of their habits and follow a pattern, analyzing which helps in discovering it. Whenever a thief steals or a robber robs a bank, he follows a pattern in committing the act of crime; whenever the police cracks the pattern, cracks the crime and nabs the criminals. Similarly, in life those who understand the pattern of human behavior can predict future acts. If their elders had followed their dark mysterious activities they could have prevented them from running away from home.

They could neither recognize him nor connect various events and facts, which they encountered then. However, they continued to gaze at him with surprise and awe. He reminded them of the incident that took place long back in their village, when on a dark night three directionless runaways were caught and sent back to their homes.

"But they were all Muslims", said Rajesh trying to reconnect the pieces in his memory, incredulously. He remembered their religion more than anything. He had painted the memories of that incident in communal colour ignorant of the fact that no religion approves bad or evil acts. For sometime, prejudices may force us to believe that the act culminated due to a particular ideology, but in the long run truth establishes that pre-judgments are hasty and without foundation.

"I am not Anis Khan."

They recalled the incident, and barely believed that either of them could have reached to such heights. They desisted from enquiring further, to clarify other facts and reconnect the old bridges, for the burden of guilt weighed heavier than their inquisitiveness and conscience. He sensed it and dispelled their difficulties by asking, "Will you not help me in my campaign now?" They accepted his offer heartily and conceded that they were already moiling for his NGO; they joined him in his campaign.

"Life moves on mysteriously, I had never expected that I would be confronted by two men, who were responsible for my return to home, when I was on the verge of going stray", thought Aditya.

"You will have to keep only one thing in mind, do not mix your religion or religious inclination in politics", said a concerned Aditya and warned them, "else I will have no other option than to chose between you and my ideals. You know what will I chose." They concurred heartily.

□

25

He made sure that he visited each and every household much before the elections. He had toiled so much for the poor masses that they called him "Bhaiya". He had conducted various workshops to ensure that every stakeholder's viewpoint was included in his election manifesto, which his friends believed to be too idealistic, whereas, his opponents thought him to be no threat for them, assuming it to be futile, and reflecting distrust in the tenets of democracy. He made himself available to the people all times when they needed any kind of help. His devotion to public life was immense and it was time that it would be tested.

One day when he sat in his room pondering over how to go about elections, he heard his inner voice tell him that people were disillusioned with his incumbent adversary, suggesting perhaps that now was the time to concentrate his energies in evolving a strategy, alive and kicking, that would educate people about the real problems.

He decided to build his campaign on twin important issues of corruption and inflation, which were intrinsically welded. He called a meeting of his supporters to explain the strategy.

"We will explain to the people how the two important issues of corruption and inflation are related."

"How is it possible?" asked one of his core team members.

"Prices increase because of two factors. When either the supply of goods reduces or demand of goods increases. In our case both the factors are at work", he explained, at which somebody requested him, " we can't understand. Please explain it in greater details."

He described, "imagine the price of vegetables that increases due to some reason. It will reduce the demand at that price level. Due to high prices, people who can't afford costly vegetables stop eating vegetables and eat something else, like pulses. It reduces the demand and price comes back to normal levels or at least the increase in price is less phenomenal."

"But, in our case income remains almost constant", someone reasoned.

He responded, "Yes, however, black money accumulated through corrupt means increases the money in the hands of a limited people. It increases their purchasing power. These limited people do not allow prices to come down as they maintain the quantity demanded at increased price level in spite of reduced or limited supply, artificially. This results in setting a new equilibrium where the prices rise more than the actual rise, had corruption not been there. Thus, prices keep on rising."

"What about workers who get good hike every year?"

"That is also responsible, though, if corruption were not there, it won't impact much. It is the poor, who eventually pays the price. We have to explain it to them and to all the honest people that if corruption is reduced the prices would not rise so much."

"It makes sense. But it will be difficult to explain ", protested another.

"We have to explain everything with examples that people understand. Tell them that due to corruption some people have more money and can afford to buy anything. Corrupt people siphon-off limited government funds meant for the poor. They will definitely understand that they were paying the price for corruption. Thus, we will ultimately bring the moral home that with reduced corruption they would be better off."

"It is a wonderful idea, we will explain it to the people in details", said Kallu zealously, who hardly understood the concept. He understood only one thing and said, "prices increase due to corruption and poor pay its price as their effective income decreases." He kept on repeating it as if to pass some exam.

"We have to ensure that people understand the link between government's failure to curb both corruption and price rise. Besides, the MLAs, who are rich do not care for the increase in price."

There was a great applause, as everybody understood that they have got a lethal weapon to fight with and a panacea to their problems. People clapped, whistled and shouted slogan for Aditya, as if they had already won the election. Reason and objectivity have no substitute. Perhaps his opponent was rich and powerful. But, he hoped that power and money could never defeat the power of reason. All that was required was communication of the real problem to the people in the language they understand.

It was a repeat of history for him. He ventured into the stranglehold of a rich man, who could have spent crores of rupees to win the election, as he was a businessman, named Krishna Agrawal. "He had made fortunes in Real Estate, Road Development, Education and Politics and won the previous elections. People believed that he had spent nearly five crore rupees in the last elections", informed Kallu.

"I have faced such person before", replied Aditya and continued, "I have lost most of the elections, but I had won my first election in the college, when there also my opponent was a carodpati. This time I will not lose."

"We have surveyed, people are disenchanted with him. He distributes money a day before voting, and those who do not fall in line are threatened", said one of his supporters and fund managers.

"We will expose him this time. We will use the power of media against him ", revealed Aditya.

"How?" asked the other one.

"Like you, there are some honest journalists who are disillusioned with him. They want to expose him. We will take their help."

"I will take them to places where corruption happens. I know the people who are involved in the distribution of money. They are his loyal people."

"But do not tell this to anyone. Do not forget that from tomorrow we have to reach the people with zeal and fireworks."

* * *

It was already evening when he was addressing a rally.

"I had always wondered why the British enslaved us and took our wealth in variety of forms and rendered us poor; now the reason was obvious – we were a lazy and irresponsible nation with no character. They took our wealth and ruined us. They ruled us with heavy hand, though they were not any different than us long back. They faced those problems two hundred years back, which we are facing now.

If the British could achieve what they wanted, why couldn't we now?" he screamed. There was applause and claps. He continued, "our time has come, the nation has awakened, and the continent has awakened, people of the world have awakened, how can we lag behind. One of my friends came back from Singapore and told me that they were worst than us sixty years back, but see today where they stand in terms of wealth and prosperity.

If they could, why can't we?" he suggested and continued, "the time is knocking at our door to awaken us from this slumber, loosing it would once again enslave us, though this time by our own people. Today we have to decide between reality and possibility. We have to decide between present and future. We need a new leadership that is inclusive and not just a preserve of the rich and powerful.

It is time to stand firm and loudly assert that we want change." He yelled once more, "We want change".

People chimed with him, vigourously, "we want change, yes, we want change". The applause and the cheer ensued in the entire gathering.

He barely finished when an entourage of supporters surrounded him with their grievances and expectations; he listened to them. When he was about to leave after taking stock of the important issues of that locality and publicity strategies with his supporters, Kallu came and informed, "Somebody wants to meet you."

"Who?"

"You better see yourself."

"Please ask him to come after I have finished listening to people."

When he finished, a dark man stood before him. He could not control his emotions; he hugged him with his eyes getting moist.

"How are you, Sayid?"

"I am fine. I came to see you when I heard you delivering the speech. I just wanted to confirm if you were really my old friend, who is fighting the election. I have designed your banners and other publicity material, hardly knowing it was for you. Had I known before, I would have made them a little more attractive."

They were very happy, both of them.

"I will pray to the Allah for your success, if you require my services and need me, you can call me anytime. I will be more than glad, to be of any help to you", he said and left. Aditya watched him leaving, the entire childhood events came huddling to his mind – childhood dreams never leave.

* * *

His supporters and volunteers put up posters, wrote on the walls, a usual bad practice during election; visited all the houses to request people to cast their votes in his favour telling them voting was democracy's success.

As planned they exposed his opponent's immoral activities before voting, several times and caught them distributing money and liquor. People who knew his opponents had decided whom to vote for. Aditya called a meeting of his workers and supporters to discuss booth level strategies and to ensure that their entire supporters vote, and are not misled by his opponent. Rajesh came running and informed that Agrawal had called a press conference.

* * *

Agrawal addressed the press conference before voting to ensure that he lived up to his character. He went for that last weapon in his armory – character assassination. "Would you like to vote for a man who ran away from his home leaving his parents? Remember this man can run away this time also, leaving you to fend for yourselves. Imagine, when you need him the most he won't be there. He has not shown the strength and inclination with which I have stood with the people of my constituency. On all occasions I have been with you. I have been elected in this constituency twice and I have not let the people down, even once. It is time for you to decide what do you want – a safe future with me, or a shaky future with someone, who runs away from his responsibilities. You must decide before you vote."

Kallu came and told Aditya about this press conference. He asked how did he know about his past.

"It is Rafiq who is campaigning with him now. He must have revealed everything to Krishna", he announced at which Rajesh was outraged at Rafiq's betrayal. Aditya restrained and convinced him that he would also call a press conference. He would address people and everything would be left for the people to decide, "Nobody should break the law, after our press conference people would have a different opinion than what Krishna wanted to project. It will seal his fate", he said and tried to convince them.

He addressed the people from the press, "It is true that I ran away from home", he revealed with such simplicity, as if making a confession, "it is also true that you may not vote for a person, who runs away every time you need him. What you were not told was that I came back and I have never run away from my responsibilities since then", he spoke from his heart – truth – plain truth. "You have a choice between the one, who ran away once and came back realizing that good could be achieved by virtue not by vice, one who believes in you and lives with you, while the other who comes as a guest in your life and deserts you after having fleeced you. You are the best judges, who will prove a good leader. Has my opponent returned after last elections? What has he done for you so far? Yes, I ran away once, but I am here to stay and serve you", he said and left.

* * *

The day of reckoning arrived; sixty percent votes were polled by the evening that was ten percent more than the previous elections. Seven days later counting would take place.

Aditya called the meeting of all his supporters and volunteers the next morning. He expressed his gratitude and said, "Whether we win or loose does not matter when we know that we have won hearts, and that is possible only because of your sustained efforts, good social work and helping in their trying times. I pray to the God that he rewards you with success for your selfless services. I shall always be grateful to you for your support."

□

26

It was the day of counting and declaration of the results. The counting was on while Aditya waited with his supporters in front of the office of the Election Officer. He thought, "I have listened to my inner voice and took another chance to see if I could achieve my cherished dream."

The election officer came out of her office to announce the result. She was searching to find the familiar face, before she could utter a word. Her eyes fell on the array of people waiting for the results and could identify what they were looking for. She peeked deeper in those eyes, as if wanted to congratulate them. Somebody shouted, "Madam who is the winner? Please tell us"; passions were running high, and the excited people were in no mood to wait. She declared Aditya to be the winner.

His supporters celebrated the victory by lifting him on their shoulders. They took him round the office campus. He had defeated one of the most influential candidates. He had lots of emotion running through his heart when Puja handed him the certificate of his election to Legislative Assembly. It appeared as if they stood on two different peaks of mountains signifying their achievements separated by an inaccessible valley. He took it and left. He turned back to see if she was still there. He was not disappointed. His heart assured, "somebody is waiting for me." He knew he could not have gone back from here now, for he had become a prisoner of that moment.

There were crackers, colours, bands, music and sweets to celebrate, but something was still missing. Kallu and Rajesh, who accompanied him, danced madly, as if they had themselves won the elections.

He finally returned back, leaving the crowd. On his return journey his entire past life stood before him, "How a small boy, a humble mother's son and a proud father's soldier had broken the myths and his own fears." He was an average boy with extraordinary determination and a capacity for perseverance. How had he achieved an impossible feat? How had he converted impossible to possible? It gave him immense satisfaction to recall how he encountered the difficult phases of his life from being a delinquent to the one, who had acquired his goal.

He understood the power of imagination, the power of a dream and the power of determination. Nothing can stop the flowers from blooming, nothing can steal the sunshine from the sun, nothing can stop talent, time and emotions that linger in the depth of the soul and find expression. It hardly matters, how difficult the paths to realize one's aim might be, one should never allow expectations to die. Only those who take risks are victors. Success might come easily for some people, but for some it does not come that easily, but, finally, it does. Failures may strike, but they should not deter efforts. Only those who try, fail, but those who fail and try again succeed. One should wait for that day. Those who never try, never succeed. It is a universal law that there is no effect without any cause. Become the cause – effect would follow.

□

Epilogue

Aditya rose to be a successful Chief Minister of the state whom the public loved and admired. After all you live in the hearts of other people also and that is your real life. Aditya's life was the journey of a dream.

Puja shifted to Delhi and never came back. She left for a foreign assignment after completing two years in Delhi; she joined UNICEF and worked for children in African countries. She was in Kenya when Parag met her the last time, while he was on a business tour to Africa. She later joined United Nations permanently.

Parag became Chief of Indian Operations of a multinational company and continued to organize get together for friends. Param after working for various companies, finally, joined Aditya and represented his party in Parliament. Neha got married and settled in Delhi with a decent job. Sam shifted to Bangalore and settled there, and Sunny after great deal of search for a spouse, finally, married and settled in France.

Sayid joined Aditya and he too became an MLA. Rafiq continued to run his shop. He apologized to Aditya, after a year of his election as MLA. Aditya lost touch with most of his school friends except Danny, who kept on visiting Dewas and updating him about others. Rajesh took over the reins to run the operations of the NGO. Kallu became councilor and assisted Aditya in managing routine local issues.

□□□